HEALING
By God's Natural Methods

1. Pure Air
2. Sunlight
3. Abstemiousness
4. Rest
5. Exercise
6. Proper Diet
7. The Use of Water
8. Trust In Divine Power

Al. Wolfsen

TEACH Services, Inc.
PUBLISHING
www.TEACHServices.com • (800) 367-1844

World rights reserved. This book or any portion thereof may not be copied or reproduced in any form or manner whatever, except as provided by law, without the written permission of the publisher, except by a reviewer who may quote brief passages in a review.

The author assumes full responsibility for the accuracy of all facts and quotations as cited in this book. The opinions expressed in this book are the author's personal views and interpretations, and do not necessarily reflect those of the publisher.

This book is provided with the understanding that the publisher is not engaged in giving spiritual, legal, medical, or other professional advice. If authoritative advice is needed, the reader should seek the counsel of a competent professional.

Copyright © 1993 TEACH Services, Inc.
ISBN-13: 978-0-945383-54-3 (Paperback)
Library of Congress Control Number: 2015910311

Abbreviations for Reference Books by Ellen G. White, a Prophet of God to the World.

CDF	*Counsels On Diet and Foods*
MH	*The Ministry of Healing*
HL	*Healthful Living*
H to L	*How to Live*
MM	*Medical Ministry*
P of H	*Place of Herbs*
1T, 2T, 3T, etc.	*Testimonies*, Vol. 1 to 9
CT & BH	*Christian Temperance & Bible Hygiene*
SA	*A Solemn Appeal*
CH	*Counsels On Health*
TS On DF	*Testimonies On Diet and Foods*
DC	*Disease and its Causes*
PP	*Patriarchs and Prophets*

"There are many ways of practicing the healing art; but there is only one way that Heaven approves." 5 T 443

This book was written by Al. Wolfsen, who was given up to die before he was 21 years old.

In 1948 he was at the point of death and the medical doctors gave up all hope of recovery. He turned away from medical "science" that offered no help and turned to the remedies found in the Bible and nature.

He prayed and promised to work for God as long as he should live. That day he had a "dream" where an angel from heaven came into the room and talked with him and took the disease away. After the "dream", he rapidly recovered.

Not forgetting his promise to work for God, as long as he should live, he has taught hundreds of sick people how to use only simple non-poisonous remedies.

He also gathered information from the American Indians, the Hawaiians, the South Sea Islands and the spanish speaking people of Mexico and Central America.

The search also led to very interesting cases of sick people who after earnest prayer to God were instructed by angels of how to get well. These remedies were carefully collected and identified.

The first part of the book is introduction to natural treatments, the rest of the book is sickness and disease listed in A, B, C, order.

DON'T DON'T DON'T
IT'S KILLING YOU

Don't use tobacco in any form.

Don't use open gas heat that can contaminate the air.

Don't allow any decay to pollute the air.

Avoid car fumes; they are poison to the lungs.

Don't breathe sprays of any kind.

Don't drink liquids with meals.

Don't drink chlorinated or fluoridated water.

Don't liquids too hot or too cold.

Don't eat fruit and vegetables at the same meal.

Don't eat anything between meals; not one bite.

Don't eat white bread.

Don't eat white flour products of any kind: pastries, donuts, macaroni, etc.

Don't use sugar or anything made from sugar.

Don't use glucose or saccharine.

Don't eat blood cooked or raw.

Don't eat fat of meat.

Don't eat grease as nucoa, lard, butter.

Don't eat embalmed foods (any preservatives added).

Don't eat food too hot or too cold.

Don't eat black pepper (cayenne is OK).

Don't eat vinegar or anything containing vinegar.

Don't eat cotton seed oil.

Don't eat candy, chocolate or cocoa.

Don't eat too much salt.

Don't overeat, even of good food.

Don't use alcohol in any form (no rubbing alcohol).

Don't drink tea or coffee.

Don't drink soft drinks, coca-cola or sodas of any kind.

Don't take aspirin or pain killers of any kind.

Don't use soda or baking powder in anything you eat.

Don't use poisonous drugs.

Don't overwork or under-exercise—balance it.

Don't stay up late at night.

Don't stay in the house too much.

Don't worry about anything: worry kills.

Don't cook or eat in aluminum.

THIS DO
AND LIVE

The temperature of the room is to be 65°. Stove heat destroys the vitality of the air and weakens the lungs.

Have a current of fresh air flow through your bedroom day and night.

The bedding should be exposed to the air daily.

Get out of doors many hours a day even in bad weather.

Breathe deeply outside several times daily till you get a little dizzy.

Keep arms and legs as warmly clad as the rest of the body.

If possible take sunbaths each week.

Drink one pint (more or less) of hot water 1/2 hour before meals.

Take two warm baths each week.

If possible take a cool bath every day.

Drink plenty of pure soft water between meals.

Eat fruit, grains, nuts and vegetables.

Keep at least 5 hours between meals and 6 hours is better.

Chew your food thoroughly, digestion begins in the mouth.

Use honey, dates, raising, etc. for sweetening.

Use honey for canning.

Milk to be only from healthy cows—then boiled, not pasteurized.

Eggs from healthy chickens cooked or raw. (Not too many.)

Eat your heavy meals at breakfast and lunch.

Eat very lightly at the evening meal (fruit and toast)

Eat evening meals several hours before bedtime.

Have meals on time at a regular time.

Take a carefree walk after meals and breathe deeply.

Have 3 or 4 dishes and no more at each meal.

Rest one full day a week (24 hours).

Three vacations a year would be fine (rest on vacations, not race).

GROW A VEGETABLE GARDEN, even if it is only 9 ft by 9 ft.

Exercise vigorously every day as you can stand it.

Believe in God and tell Him your troubles.

The Laws

Tables of Stone written with the Finger of God

I
Thou shalt have no other Gods before me.

II
Thou shalt not make unto thee any graven image, or any likeness of any thing that is in heaven above, or that is in the earth beneath, or that is in the water under the earth: Thou shalt not bow down thyself to them, nor serve them: for I the LORD thy God am a jealous God, visiting the iniquity of the fathers upon the children unto the third and fourth generation of them that hate me; and shewing mercy unto thousands of them that love me, and keep my commandments.

III
Thou shalt not take the name of the LORD thy God in vain; for the LORD will not hold him guiltless that taketh his name in vain.

IV
Remember the sabbath day, to keep it holy. Six days shalt thou labour, and do all thy work: but the seventh day is the sabbath of the LORD thy God: in it thou shalt not do any work, thou, nor thy son, nor thy daughter, thy manservant, nor thy maidservant, nor thy cattle, nor thy stranger that is within thy gates: For in six days the LORD made heaven and earth, the sea, and all that in them is, and rested the seventh day: wherefore the LORD blessed the sabbath day, and hallowed it.

V
Honour thy Father and thy Mother: that thy days may be long upon the land which the LORD thy God giveth thee.

VI
Thou shalt not kill.

VII
Thou shalt not commit adultery.

VIII
Thou shalt not steal.

IX
Thou shalt not bear false witness against thy neighbor.

X
Thou shalt not covet thy neighbor's house, thou shalt not covet thy neighbor's wife, nor his manservant, nor his maidservant, nor his ox, nor his ass, nor any thing that is thy neighbor's.

the Moral Law

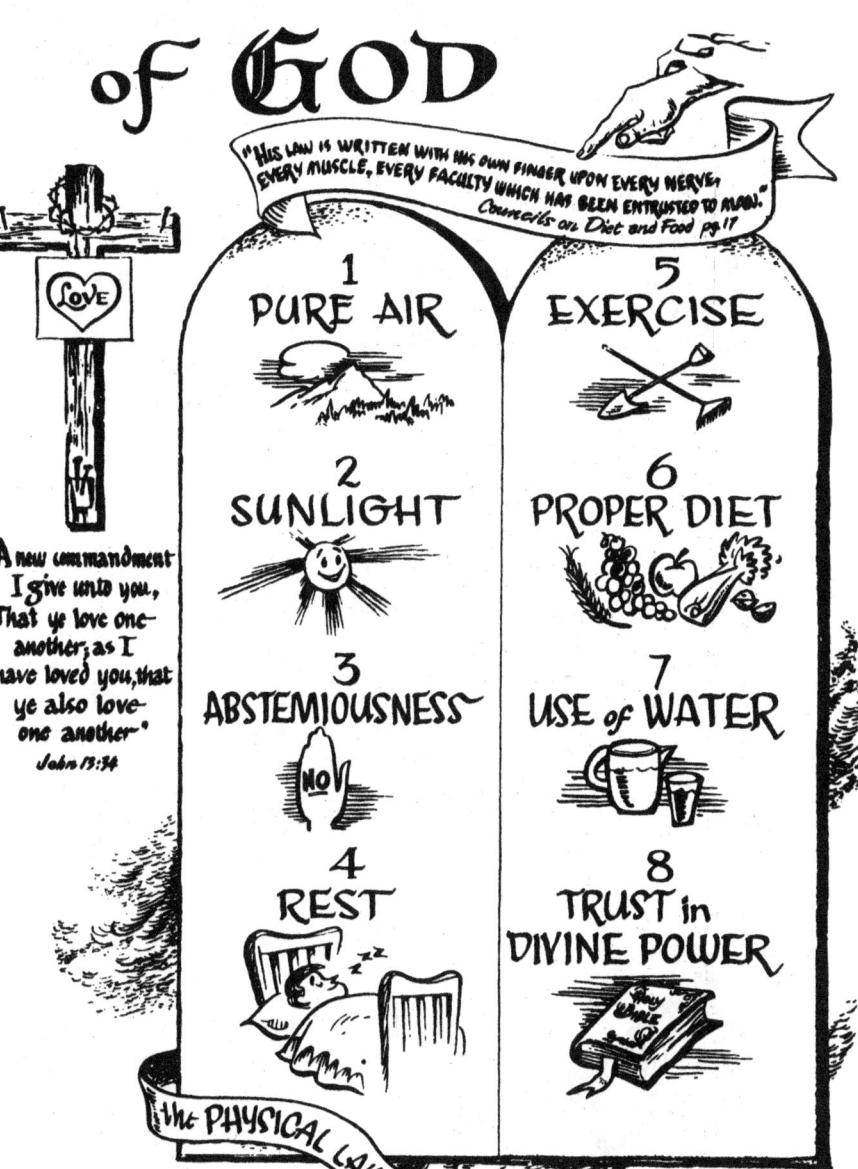

INTRODUCTION

If you are sick the way you have lived, the way you have worked, the way you have played, the way you have eaten, the way you have drunk, the way you have slept, the kind of air you are breathing, the kind of thoughts you are thinking, the kind of people you choose as friends, the hours you keep, any and all of these things are things that add up to sickness or health.

"God has formed laws which govern our constitutions and these laws which He has placed in our being are divine, and for every transgression there is affixed a penalty, which must sooner or later be realized. The majority of disease which the human family have been and still are suffering under, they have created by ignorance of their own organic laws." CDF 17.

"God is as truly the author of physical laws as He is author of the moral law. His law is written with His own finger upon every nerve, every muscle, every faculty which has been entrusted to man." CDF 17.

"Dearly beloved, let us cleanse ourselves from all filthiness of the flesh and spirit, perfecting holiness in the fear of God." II Cor. 7:1.

DISEASE

"It is as truly a sin to violate the laws of our being as it is to break the ten commandments, to do either is to break God's laws." "To keep the body in a healthy condition, in order that all parts of the living machinery may act harmoniously, should be a study of our life." CDF 17.

"My people are destroyed for lack of knowledge." Hosea 4:6.

You can do for yourself what no other person in this world can do for you, CHANGE YOUR HABITS. This must be done by you alone.

Don't annoy others around you by your changes in your habits of living, but make the changes as quietly as possible. Don't try to break others of their health destroying habits around you, as that will only make them angry. Take such good care of your health that others will come to you and ask how you do it, then tell them a little.

DISEASE

In case of sickness, the cause should be ascertained, unhealthful conditions should be changed, wrong habits corrected. Then nature is to be assisted in her effort to expel impurities and to reestablish right conditions in the system. MH 127.

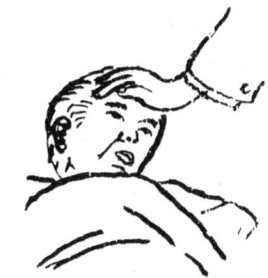

Disease is not a thing. It is the absence of a thing—health.

DISEASE

Disease is the effort of nature to sweep out the dirt from the body that has been brought in by our ignorance of the laws of health.

Disease is inside dirt that nature is sweeping out.

Disease! Is it a friend, or is it an enemy?

Disease is an effort of nature to free the system from conditions that result from a violation of the laws of health.

If disease is an effort of nature to get the rubbish or toxic poisons out of our bodies, we don't want to kill the disease that is sweeping out trash and rubbish from the body but help nature do the job of house cleaning.

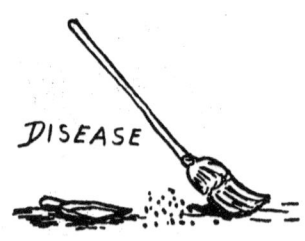

"Nature, to relieve herself of poisonous impurities, makes an effort to free the system, which effort produces fevers and what is termed disease, but even then if those who are afflicted would assist nature in her efforts by the use pure, soft water, much suffering would be prevented." HL 977.

DISEASE

A COLD is a good example of many diseases. The white stuff (and later the yellow or greenish mucous-snot) which comes from the

nose and lungs is the toxin or dirt. This has piled up deeply inside and has produced a dirty body. The cold is the effort of nature to clean house. You do not catch a cold from the air, or from someone else. You have clogged your body with sugar, starches, refined foods, insufficient clothes or staying up too late at night. The cold is the effort of nature to unload the garbage can.

Many don't know they are breaking the laws of health and need instruction.

A practice that is laying the foundation of a vast amount of disease and of even more serious evils, is the free use of poisonous drugs. People need to be taught that they sometimes afford present relief, and the patient appears to recover as the result of their use; this is because nature has sufficient vital force to expel the poison and to correct the conditions that caused the disease. Health is recovered in spite of the drug.

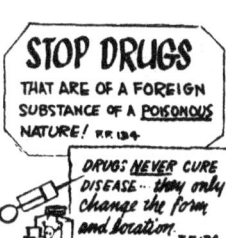

8 LAWS OF HEALTH

But in most cases the drug only changes the form and location of the disease. Often the effect of the poison seems to be overcome for a time, but the results remain the system, and work great harm at some later period.

By the use of poisonous drugs, many bring upon themselves lifelong illness, and many lives are lost that might be saved by the use of natural methods of healing.

"Patients are to be supplied with good, wholesome food; total abstinence from all intoxicating drinks is to be observed; drugs are to be discarded, and rational methods of treatment followed. The patient must not be given alcohol, tea, coffee, or drugs; for these always leave traces of evil behind them. By observing these rules, many who have been given up by the physicians may be restored to health." MM 228.

8 LAWS OF HEALTH
NATURAL REMEDIES

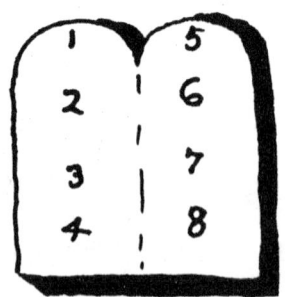

"Pure air, sunlight, abstemiousness, rest, exercise, proper diet, the use of water, trust in divine power—these are the true remedies. Every person should have a knowledge of nature's remedial agencies and how to apply them. MH 127.

AIR

8 LAWS OF HEALTH

PURE AIR

"And the Lord God formed man of the dust of the ground and breathed into his nostrils the breath of life; and man became a living soul." Gen. 2:7.

"Air is the free blessing of heaven, calculated to electrify the whole system. Without it the system will be filled with disease, and become dormant, languid, feeble, yet you have all been for years living with a very limited amount of air." 1T 701.

"Stove heat destroys the vitality of the air and weakens the lungs." P of H, p. 9.

AN OPEN FIRE IS BEST

"In order to maintain equal circulation, there should be equal distribution of clothing, which will bring equal warmth to all parts of the body." HL 307.

Get out of doors many hours a day even in bad weather. Breathe deeply outside several times a day. Have a current of fresh air flow through your bedroom day and night. The bedding should be exposed to the air daily. The temperature of rooms should not be above 65 degrees in winter. Keep arms and legs as warmly clad as the rest of the body.

8 LAWS OF HEALTH

"To secure a good circulation of the current of human life, all parts of the body must be suitably clad." HL 788.

Air out the bed all day every day and put all the bedding out in the sunshine and air often.

"Fresh air will prove more beneficial to the sick than medicine, and is far more essential to them than their food." HL 652.

Don't allow any decay to pollute the air around the house.

Don't use open gas heat that can contaminate the air.

Avoid car fumes; they are poison to the lungs.

Don't breathe poison sprays of any kind.

Move out of a smog area. Get into the hills and live from the soil.

—PURE

There is health in the fragrance of the pine, the cedar and the fir. And there are several other kinds of trees that have medicinal properties that are health promoting.

8 LAWS OF HEALTH

"Mothers dress their children with limbs nearly naked; and the blood is chilled back from its natural course and thrown upon the internal organs, breaking up the circulation and producing disease."

Move out of the cities. Get into the country. Make a garden. Live from the soil. Build your own house. Teach your children how to grow food, and how to work at trades.

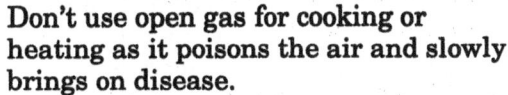

Get into the hills and mountains. Avoid automobile exhaust, filthy smells of decay and tobacco.

Don't use open gas for cooking or heating as it poisons the air and slowly brings on disease.

Use wood heat and have a fireplace to get the canned sunshine from the burning wood in winter.

Open your doors and windows and let the fresh air in. In cool or cold weather put on nice warm clothes that protect the arms and legs from chilliness keeping them as warm as your forehead. Feel of your ankles and your wrists and notice if they are colder than your forehead, if they are you are doing a lot of damage to your health.

8 LAWS OF HEALTH

Soft lambs wool makes the very best clothing for cold weather. Cotton is good also.
Spend a lot of your time out of doors in the fresh air summer and winter.
Take walks outdoors even in bad weather.
Go barefoot if possible. It quiets the nerves and promotes health.

If you get cold the best way to warm up is to do some strong work or exercise.
If you must warm up, an open fireplace is the best kind heat. THEN EXERCISE. TAKE A WALK.

SUNLIGHT

Come out in the sunshine and gather its wealth; there is joy in the sunshine and beauty and health; why stay in the shadows, why sit in the gloom, come out in the sunshine and blossom and bloom. So goes the words of an old song.

For good health build your home on high dry ground with shade trees and vines kept far enough away to let in plenty of sunshine all around the house.

8 LAWS OF HEALTH

The best substitute for sunshine in winter is the open fire in a camp fire or fireplace of burning wood, the canned sunshine in the wood is released into you.

The confined air of unventilated rooms meets us with sickening odors of mildew and mold, and the impurities exhaled from its inmates. The emanations from damp moldy rooms and clothing are poisonous to the system.

SUN BATH

The feeble one should press out into the sunshine as earnestly and naturally as do the shaded plants and vines.

Go out into the light and warmth of the glorious sun, you pale and sickly ones, and share with vegetation its life-giving, health dealing power.

FACE THE SUN

½" CELOTEX OR PLYWOOD

EVERYONE SICK OR WELL NEEDS SUN-BATHS.

BUILD ONE.

I must get all the sunlight that it is possible for me to obtain. P of H 3. The blood is increased 25 percent by sunbaths.

In taking sunbaths begin very slowly with 1 or 2 minutes on each side. Then increase the length of time one or 2 minutes each day. Don't let your skin burn.

8 LAWS OF HEALTH

Sunshine that is filtered through glass has lost its health and life giving power. Plastic lets the healing rays through to you. The best is pure sunshine.

If you would have your homes sweet and inviting make them bright with air and sunshine. Remove your heavy curtains, open the windows.

Sunlight is one of nature's most healing agents.

—COLORS

GREEN—relaxes the body and mind

RED—Courage, warmth, stimulating too much red is not good. Have just a dot of red here and there.

YELLOW—is a nerve builder. Very healing color

BLUE—is a cooling color

The colors in nature are always in balance.

To the sick it is worth more than silver and gold to lie in the sunshine or in the shade of the trees. 7T 85.

Pure air, good water, sunshine, the beautiful surroundings of nature ... these are His (God's) means for restoring the sick to health. 7T 85.

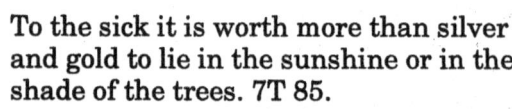

8 LAWS OF HEALTH

ABSTEMIOUSNESS

DON'T, DON'T, DON'T, IT'S KILLING YOU.

Don't use *tobacco* in any form. It's a slow poison.

Stop the use of *alcohol*. No good.

Stay away from all poisonous *drugs*. They kill.

Don't drink *tea* nor *coffee*. It ruins the nerves.

Stop *sugar* water drinks, sodas. It clogs the system.

Don't use *sugar* in any form. Use honey, fruits.

No *candy*, ice cream, cake. It rots the teeth.

No chewing gum. It is full of sugar.

No pork. It is unclean. Leviticus 7, 11.

Don't eat any blood, or you are guilty of murder. Gen. 9:4, 5.

Don't use grease or butter. It greases the bowels. Cheese should not enter the stomach. It binds up the bowels.

Don't eat between meals. Nothing except water.

Keep a full 5 or 6 hours in between meals. Ruins digestion if you don't.

Don't cook or eat in aluminum. It poisons the food.

Don't use foods that are taken apart. They starve you. White flour, white rice, white sugar starve you. White bread, causes disease, constipation. Yeast causes fermentation in the stomach. Baking powder poisons the stomach. Soda eats the lining from the stomach. Vinegar stops healing. Black pepper is bad for heart and stomach, nerves. Red hot cayenne pepper heals heart and stomach. Don't use aspirin or tranquilizers, pain killers. They ruin the nerves.

8 LAWS OF HEALTH

Open gas heat contaminates the air.

Don't allow any decay to pollute the air.

Avoid car exhaust, it poisons the lungs.

Don't breathe spray of any kind. It kills.

Don't drink liquids with meals. Use your saliva.

Don't drink chlorinated or fluoridated water.

Don't eat or drink foods too hot or too cold. Hot foods cause cancer of the throat. Cold foods slow down digestion.

Avoid fruits and vegetables at same meal.

Don't have too many varieties at one meal.

Molasses and syrups clog the blood stream.

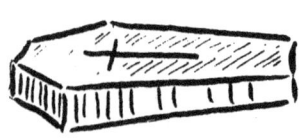

Stay away from food preservatives. They are poison.

Chocolate and cocoa are stimulants. Don't use them.

Salt refined causes sickness.

Use sea water dried.

Don't overeat, even of good food.

Don't under exercise or over work, balance it.

Don't stay up late at night.

Go to bed at dark and get up early to study, read.

Don't worry about anything; worry kills. Worry is the inability to make a decision. Make decisions and clear your mind even if you are wrong. If you are wrong change it.

Hypnosis weakens the mind, stay away from it.

"Thou shalt not commit adultery" Ex. 20:14.

Warning: stop sex enervation.

8 LAWS OF HEALTH

"A failure to care for the living machinery is an insult to the creator. There are divinely appointed rules which if observed, will keep human beings from disease and premature death." CDF 16.

—FLESH MEATS

"The liability to disease is increased by flesh-eating. We do not hesitate to say that meat is not essential to the maintenance to health and strength." CT&BH 47.

UNCLEAN MEATS

PASSION

"Thou shalt not commit adultery! Exodus 20.

The unholy cannot enter the kingdom of heaven—"Neither fornicators, nor idolaters, nor effeminate (those guilty of self-abuse) nor abusers of themselves with mankind." I Cor. 6:9.

"Dearly beloved, I beseech you as strangers and pilgrims abstain from fleshly lusts which war against the soul." I Pet. 2:9, 11.

"Let us first view the results of this vice upon the physical strength. Have you not marked the lack of healthful beauty, of strength and power of endurance in your dear children.

8 LAWS OF HEALTH

Have you not felt saddened as you have watched the progress of disease upon them, which has baffled your skill, and that of physicians? You listen to numerous complaints of headache, catarrh, dizziness, nervousness, pain in the shoulders and sides, loss of appetite, pain in the back and limbs, wakeful, feverish nights, of tired feelings in the morning, and great exhaustion after exercising? As you have seen the beauty of health disappearing and have marked the sallow countenance, or the unnaturally flushed face, have you been sufficiently aroused to look beneath the surface, to inquire into the cause of this physical decay? Have you observed the astonishing mortality among the youth? And have you not noticed that there was a deficiency in mental health of your children? That their course seemed to be marked with extremes? That they were absent-minded? That they started nervously when spoken to? And were easily irritated?

Have you not noticed that, when occupied upon a piece of work they would look dreamingly, as though the mind was elsewhere? And when they came to their senses, they were unwilling to own the work as coming from their hands, it was so full of mistakes, and showed such marks of inattention? Have you not been astonished at their wonderful forgetfulness?

8 LAWS OF HEALTH

3 ABSTEMIOUSNESS

The most simple and oft-repeated directions would be forgotten, sieve-like memories. Have you not noticed their reluctance to engage in active labour? The tendency of many is to live in indolence. SA 1-7.

"Have you not witnessed the gloomy sadness upon the countenance, and frequent exhibitions of morose temper in those who once were cheerful, kind and affectionate? They are easily excited to jealousy, disposed to look upon the dark side, and when you are labouring for their good, imagine that you are their enemy, that you needlessly reprove and restrain them. Have you not noticed the increase of disobedience in children, and their ingratitude and impatience under restraint? SA 1-7.

"Have you not felt distressed and anxious as you have seen the strong desire in your children to be with the other sex. Blind passion overrules sensible considerations.

"They follow their willful course and are controlled by perhaps a premature marriage, or are brought to shame. Boys and girls enter upon the marriage relation with unripe love and immature judgment." SA 1-7.

8 LAWS OF HEALTH

"The less feverish the diet, the more easily can the passions be controlled." 2T 352.

"Industry does not weary and exhaust one fifth (1/5) as much as the pernicious habit of self-abuse." HL 940

"Vice after 15 years of age will pay penalty for transgression of her laws especially from ages of thirty to forty-five, by numerous pains in the system such as, afflictions of liver, lungs, neuralgia, rheumatism, affection of spine, diseased kidneys, cancerous tumors." SA 19.

"The body is enervated, the brain is weakened. The material there deposited to nourish the system is squandered. The drain upon the system is great. SA 40.

"God requires them to control their married lives from any excesses. But very few feel it to be a religious duty to govern their passions. They reason that marriage sanctifies the indulgence of the baser passions. God holds them accountable for the expenditure of vital energy, which weakens their hold on life and enervates the entire system." SA 43.

8 LAWS OF HEALTH

"Youth should not marry aged. Old men should not marry young wives, still worse for young men to marry old women. The offspring of such unions in many cases, where ages widely differ, have not well-balanced minds." SA 67

REST

Rest every part of your body.

Your hearts rests at the end of each beat.

Your lungs rest at the end of each breath.

Rest your stomach for one hour before the next meal.

Go to bed at dark, the hours before midnight are the most valuable for rest and body building.

If you must work at night, do it early in the morning, but get your sleep before midnight.

Rest one day every week. Ex. 20:8-11 "Remember."

Three vacations a year would be fine.

After 6 years work take the 7th year off. Lev. 25:1-8.

"When we lie down at night, the stomach should have its work all done, that it, as well as other portions of the body may enjoy rest." CT&BH 50.

One hour of sleep before midnight is worth 4 hours of sleep after midnight. One hour of work early in the morning is worth 4 hours of work before midnight.

8 LAWS OF HEALTH

"And on the seventh day God ended His work which He had made (creation); and He rested on the seventh day from all His work which He had made. And God blessed the seventh day and sanctified it: because that in it He had rested from all His work which God created and made." Gen. 2:2, 3.

"A merry heart doeth good like a medicine. But a broken spirit drieth the bones." Prov. 17:22.

"Let not your heart be troubled: ye believe in God." John 14:1.

"Remember the Sabbath day to keep it holy. Six days shalt thou labour, and do all thy work.... Exodus 20: 8, 9.

The mind must rest.

"For as he thinketh in his heart, so is he."

Make up your mind and then relax. Worry is thinking of your problem and never bringing your mind to a decision.

Practice relaxing right now. Let every muscle in your body go limp. Do this every time you get tense. Then work with every muscle as loose as possible. While working practice and think how to do each little job a little better and a little faster, a little neater and it will be much easier. Use only as much muscle tension as is necessary to do the job but let all other muscles be relaxed. Then you can accomplish 5 times more work without getting tired.

8 LAWS OF HEALTH

"That which brings sickness of body and mind to nearly all is dissatisfied feelings and discontented repinings." HL 997.

"Sickness of the mind prevails everywhere. Nine tenths (90%) of the diseases from which men suffer have their foundation here." HL 987.

"The sympathy which exists between the mind and the body is very great, when one is affected, the other responds." 4T 60.

"In nine cases out of ten, the knowledge of a sin pardoning Saviour would make them better both in mind and body." HL 1009.

Eyes: Be careful to have the light coming over your left shoulder on your reading or your work. Not into your eyes. Fluorescent lights ruin the eyes as they blink on and off 60 times a second.

When reading or looking at something look at the spot in the center of your vision not to the side. Don't look ahead as you read but look at the word you are reading. To strengthen your eyes, read one page with one eye and the next page with the other.

Mind Breakdown—"The main cause is improper diet, irregular meals, and a lack of physical exercise. Irregular hours for eating and sleeping sap the brain forces." HL 847.

8 LAWS OF HEALTH

"Nothing is so fruitful a cause of disease as depression, gloominess and sadness." HL 996.

Worry ends where faith in God begins.

EXERCISE

More people rust out then wear out.

"Thousands are sick and dying around us who might get well and live if they would; but their imagination holds them. They fear that they will be made worse if they labor or exercise, when this is just the change they need to make them well. Without this, they never can improve. They should exercise the power of the will, rise above their aches and debility, and engage in useful employment and forget that they have aching backs, sides, lungs and heads." 3T 76.

Exercise, and free and abundant use of the air and sunlight would give life and strength to the emaciated. HL 982.

"Morning exercise, in walking in the free invigorating air of heaven is the surest safeguard against colds, coughs, congestions of the brain and lungs.... and a hundred other diseases." HL 903.

8 LAWS OF HEALTH

"There is no exercise that will prove as beneficial to every part of the body as walking." HL 572.

"If physical exercise were combined with mental exertion, the blood would be quickened in its circulation, the action of the heart would be more perfect, impure matter would be thrown off, and new life and vigor would be experienced in every part of the body." 3T 490.

"Active walking in the open air will do more for women, to preserve them in health if they are well than any other means." HL 572.

Exercise as vigorously every day as you can. Sweat every day. Gen. 3:19 "The sweat of thy face." Exercise every part of your body every day.

EXERCISE SUMMER AND WINTER

"A walk, even in winter, would be more beneficial to the health than all the medicine the doctors may prescribe." HL 571.

"Take time to cultivate your gardens, thus gaining the exercise needed to keep the system in good working order." HL 566.

27

8 LAWS OF HEALTH

"Neglecting to exercise the entire body, or a portion of it, will bring on morbid conditions, and will cause the blood to flow sluggishly through the blood vessels." 3T 76.

"The true glory and joy of life are found only by the working man and woman. Labor brings its own reward, and sweet is the rest that is purchased by the fatigue of a well-spent day." CT & BH 98.

"As a rule, the labor of the day should not be prolonged into the evening. Let parents devote the evenings to their families." CT & BH 65.

DON'T OVERWORK or UNDER-EXERCISE, BALANCE IT.

"In the use of rake and hoe and spade they will find relief for many of their maladies. Idleness is the cause of many diseases. Life in the open air is good for body and mind. It is God's medicine for the restoration of health.

"Each faculty of the mind and each muscle has its distinctive office, and all require to be exercised in order to become properly developed and retain healthful vigor." HL 819.

"Self-made invalids, dying by inches, dying of indolence, a disease which no one but themselves can cure." HL 594.

8 LAWS OF HEALTH

"Neglecting to exercise the entire body, or a portion of it, will bring on morbid conditions." HL 595.

"Continued inactivity is one of the greatest causes of debility of body and feebleness of mind." HL 597.

"Neither study nor violent exercise should be engaged in immediately after a full meal. When mind or body is taxed heavily after eating, the process of digestion is hindered." HL 576.

"God designed that the living machinery should be in daily activity; for in this activity or motion is its preserving power." HL 577.

"By active exercise in the open air every day the liver, kidneys, and lungs also will be strengthened to perform their work." HL 578.

"A large class of women are content to hover over the stove, breathing impure air for one-half or three-quarters of the time, until the brain is heated and one-half benumbed. They should go out and exercise every day even though some things indoors have to be neglected. They need the cool air to quiet distracted brains." HL 575.

8 LAWS OF HEALTH

THIN OR OVERWEIGHT

"They closely apply their minds to books, and eat the allowance of a laboring man. Under such habits some grow corpulent, because the system is clogged, others become lean, feeble, and weak, because their vital powers are exhausted in throwing off the excess of food." 3T 490.

"Exercise will aid the work of digestion. To walk out after a meal, hold the head erect, put back the shoulders, and exercise moderately, will be a great benefit. The mind will be diverted from self to the beauties of nature." HL 573.

 ## PROPER DIET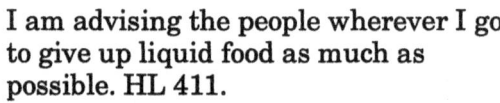

FOODS—LIQUID

I am advising the people wherever I go to give up liquid food as much as possible. HL 411.

You should use the most simple food, prepared in the most simple manner. CH 63.

Dry food which requires mastication is far preferable to porridges (mush). HL 351.

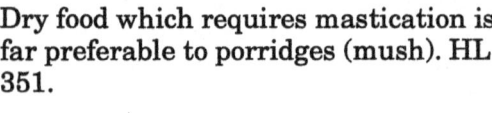

Food should be thoroughly cooked, nicely prepared, and appetizing. HL 355.

8 LAWS OF HEALTH

If the third meal be eaten at all, it should be light, and several hours before going to bed. HL 385.

Grow a garden. This do and live, even if it is only 9 feet by 9 feet.

Eat fruits, grains, nuts, vegetables for best health.

Keep at least 5 hours between meals 6 hours better.

Chew your food thoroughly, digestion begins in the mouth. Eat your heavy meals at breakfast and lunch. Eat very lightly at the evening meal or none at all. Eat evening meals several hours before bedtime. Have your meals on time at a regular time. Take a carefree walk after meals and breathe deeply.

Use honey, dates, raisins, etc. for sweetening. Use honey for canning, not sugar.

In place of grease use oil of some kind, olive oil, sesame oil, peanut oil, etc.

Use fresh healthy milk for babies or banana and coconut milk. For adults healthy milk soured naturally is best. Be sure the cow or goat is not sick. Eggs from healthy chickens (not too many).

Drink one pint (more or less) of hot water 1/2 hour before meals.

DIET—CHILDREN

They should be allowed only plain food, and that should be partaken of only at regular periods, not oftener than three times a day, and two meals would be better than three. SA 86

RIPE BANANA WITH GRATED COCONUT. POUR HOT WATER OVER GRATED COCONUT AND SQUEEZE THROUGH A CLOTH. MIX WITH RIPE BANANA FOR BABY'S MILK. THEY GROW WONDERFULY ON THIS MILK.

8 LAWS OF HEALTH

"Very hot food ought not to be taken into the stomach. Let them become partly cooled before they are eaten." HL 414.

DIET

"Fruits, grains, nuts and vegetables, prepared in a simple way, free from spice and grease of all kinds, make with milk the most healthful diet." HL 348.

"You should use the most simple food, prepared in the most simple manner." 2T 46.

"Food should be thoroughly cooked, nicely prepared, and appetizing." HL 354.

Nearly all the members of the human family eat more than the system requires. If more food, even of a simple quantity, is placed in the stomach then the living machinery requires, this surplus becomes a burden. HL 400.

Food should not be washed down, no drink is needed with meals. Eat slowly, and allow the saliva to mingle with the food. HL 410.

If the extras which are provided for dessert were dispensed with altogether, it would be a blessing. HL 417.

"Regularity in eating is very important for health of body and serenity of mind. Never should a morsel of food pass the lips between meals." CT & BH 50.

8 LAWS OF HEALTH

"Five hours at least should be given between each meal, and always bear in mind that if you would give it a trial, you would find that two meals would be better than three." HL 678.

"Flesh meats will depreciate the blood. Cook meat with spices, and eat it with rich cakes and pies, and you have a bad quality of blood. The system is too heavily taxed in disposing of this kind of food." HL 760.

"Those who are excited, anxious, or in a hurry, would do well not to eat until they have found rest or relief." CT & BH 52.

"Hot drinks are debilitating; and besides, those who indulge in their use become slaves to the habit." HL 673.

"Taken with meals, water diminishes the flow of the salivary glands, and the colder the water, the greater the injury to the stomach." HL 672.

8 LAWS OF HEALTH

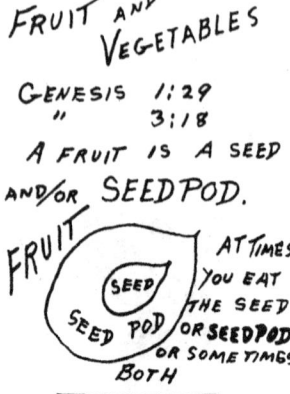

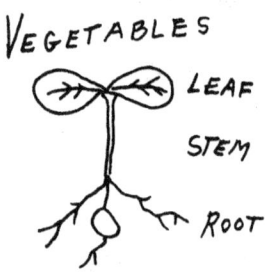

—OVEREATING

"Indulging in eating too frequently, and of too large quantities, overtaxes the digestive organs produces a feverish state of the system. The blood becomes impure, and then diseases of various kinds follow." HL 755.

—FRUIT AND VEGETABLES

"If we would preserve the best health, we should avoid eating vegetables and fruit at the same meal. If the stomach is feeble, there will be distress, and the brain will be confused, and unable to put forth mental effort. HAVE FRUIT AT ONE MEAL AND VEGETABLES AT THE NEXT. HL 376.

—FOOD AND FEVERS

"While fever is raging, food may irritate and excite the blood; but as soon as the strength of the fever is broken, nourishment should be given in careful, judicious manner." HL 759.

—TIME IN MOUTH

"The benefit derived from food does not depend so much on the quantity eaten, as on its thorough digestion; nor the gratification of taste so much on the amount of food swallowed, as on the length of time it remains in the mouth." CT & BH 52.

"Masticate slowly, and allow the saliva to mingle with the food." CT & BH 51.

"Thorough mastication is a benefit both to the teeth and the stomach." HL 664.

8 LAWS OF HEALTH

—BREADS

"Hot biscuits raised with soda or baking powder should never appear upon our tables. Such compounds are unfit to enter the stomach. Hot raised bread of any kind is difficult to digestion."

For use in breadmaking, the super fine white flour is not the best. It is a frequent cause of constipation and other unhealthful conditions.

The use of soda or baking powder in breadmaking is harmful and unnecessary.

Soda eats the coating of the stomach.

—DON'T TAKE IT APART

"What therefore God hath joined together, let not man put asunder." Matt. 19:6.

A BIRD WITH ONE SHORT WING CAN'T FLY. IT'S OUT OF BALANCE.
FOOD THAT HAS BEEN TAKEN APART IS OUT OF BALANCE.

Don't take apart wheat, corn, rice, barley, sugar, salt, herbs.

Wheat, in small amounts is a good food made into a variety of good things to eat if it is not taken apart by milling and refining, and separating the white flour from the bran the oil, the germ. White flour is the cause of many diseases. Use whole wheat. Rice is the food of many people, but it should never be polished as polishing rice destroys much of the food value and is the cause of scurvy, rickets, sore joints and many other diseases. Use brown rice.

8 LAWS OF HEALTH

All grains and foods should be eaten with nothing taken away if it is possible to eat it. Grape skins and seeds. Unsprayed apples eat them skin and all. Carrots washed but not scraped are best. Potatoes should never have the skins peeled off. Eat it all. Swallow water melon seeds whole or chew them up, but don't spit them out.

Corn is a good food and is the gold of Mexico but do not put lime on it to remove the outer covering and the germ of life and the oil.

—BREAD

"Bread should be light and sweet. Not the least taint of sourness should be tolerated. The loaves should be small, and so thoroughly baked that, so far as possible the yeast germs shall be destroyed. When hot, or new, raised bread of any kind is difficult of digestion. It should never appear on the table. This rule does not, however, apply to unleavened bread. Fresh rolls made of wheaten meal (whole grains) without yeast or leaven and baked in a well heated oven are both wholesome and palatable." TS & DF 10.

—CHEESE

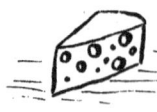

"The effect of cheese is deleterious. Cheese should never be introduced into the stomach." HL 425.

Cottage cheese is often worse than any other kind of cheese because of the old milk used in making it and the preservatives added to make it keep along time in the store.

8 LAWS OF HEALTH

—DON'T USE SUGAR—USE HONEY

"The free use of sugar in any form tends to clog the system, and is not infrequently a cause of disease." HL 264.

"Sugar, when largely used, is more injurious than meat." 2 T 370.

—MILK AND EGGS

Use milk only from healthy cows or goats.

Use eggs from healthy chickens, properly cared for and suitably fed.

"The time will soon come when there will be no safety in using eggs." TS DF 120.

"We may not long be able to use even milk." HL 349.

"When you see that you are becoming weak physically, it is essential for you to make changes, and at once." TS DF 401.

—SPROUTS

Sprouted seeds are the most powerful food in the world. Sprouted seeds are 400 to 500 times more powerful as food than any other food in this world, the tests show.

Daniel in the Bible ate sprouts (pulse) and at the end of ten days their faces appeared fairer and fatter than all the others. Also they were the wisest of all the wise men in Babylon and became the king's counselors. Dan. 1.

SPROUT SEEDS THIS WAY

JAR LID RING

CUT SCREEN TO FIT

GLASS JAR

PUT SEEDS TO SPROUT IN JAR. SOAK IN WATER OVER NIGHT.

RINSE SEEDS TWICE DAILY.

GROW SEEDS WITH JAR UPSIDE DOWN TO DRAIN OFF ALL WATER.

8 LAWS OF HEALTH

SUGAR—is a good food in the sugar cane or sugar beet, but taken apart with the molasses removed and a lot of refining it becomes a poisonous load to clog up the blood stream, gives pain of the muscles and joints, called rheumatism, and arthritis, hardening of the arteries, heart trouble and the common cold, pneumonia, polio, diabetes, sickness of many kinds and many deaths need not be. Don't use sugar in any form. Use honey, or sugar cane.

SALT—Salt is very necessary to the blood stream and should be used just as God made it in the ocean or dried sea water with none of the 97 elements removed except the water. It is very important that none of these elements be changed or taken apart. Yet table salt in most cases has nearly all of the 97 elements removed. This causes hardening of the arteries, edema, heart troubles, malnutrition, hidden hunger, eye trouble.

Use sea water to salt your foods with a little lemon juice it is wonderful on salads.

—HERBS FOR MEDICINE

Don't take them apart. "What therefore God hath joined together, let not man put asunder." Matt. 19:6. Whenever man takes a good herb and extracts some part for medicine he has ruined it and it does not do the job of healing. Leave it alone.

8 LAWS OF HEALTH

Gather your herbs for medicine, dry them in the shade. Use them whole for sickness make a cup of herb tea by pouring boiling water over a little of the herbs in a cup. Let stand till cool enough to drink and it will do wonders.

—RAW FOODS

When possible eat foods fresh, ripe, unsprayed, grown with natural fertilizers. For people with all kinds of hard incurable diseases a diet of raw food, unheated, never cooked, processed or taken apart will give nature just what is needed to recover health from nearly every disease. Try it for 30 days. Eat fruits, grains, nuts, vegetables. Keep a full 6 hours in between your meals and eat or drink nothing. Use sea weeds daily on this program.

STOMACH

All that is taken into the stomach, above what the system can use to convert into good blood, clogs the machinery. For it cannot be made into either flesh or blood and its presence burdens the liver. CH page 160.

The more you feed a sick person the more you harm him. Hippocrates.

Your food shall be your remedies and your remedies shall be your food.

8 LAWS OF HEALTH

WATER

"There are many ways in which water can be applied to relieve pain and check disease. All should become intelligent in its use in simple home treatments. Mothers especially, should know how to care for their families in both health and sickness." MH 237.

Drink plenty of pure soft water between meals. Take two warm baths each week. If possible take a cool bath every day.

"In health and in sickness, pure water is one of heaven's choicest blessings. Its proper use promotes health. It is the beverage which God provided to quench the thirst of animals and man. Drunk freely, it helps to supply the necessities of the system, and assist nature to resist disease. The external application of water is one of the easiest and most satisfactory ways of regulating the circulation of the blood. A cold or cool bath is an excellent tonic. Warm baths open the pores, and thus aid in the elimination of impurities. But warm and neutral baths soothe the nerves and equalize the circulation." MH 237.

8 LAWS OF HEALTH

—TREATMENT

Fast for one or two meals, and drink only pure, soft water. The loss of a meal or two will enable the overburdened system to overcome slight indispositions, and even graver difficulties may sometimes be overcome by this simple process. HL 963.

—SEA WATER

For constipation

For burns

For minerals

For blood deficiencies

For pregnancies

For babies

For hidden hunger.

"Thousands have died for want of pure water, and pure air, who might have lived, and thousands of invalids, who are a burden to themselves and others, think that their lives depend upon taking medicines from the doctors. They are continually guarding themselves against the air, and avoiding the use of water. These blessings they need in order to become well. If they would become enlightened, and let medicine alone, and accustom themselves to outdoor exercise and to air in their houses, summer and winter, and use soft water for drinking and bathing purposes, they would be comparatively well and happy." CH 55.

8 LAWS OF HEALTH

—THE USE OF WATER

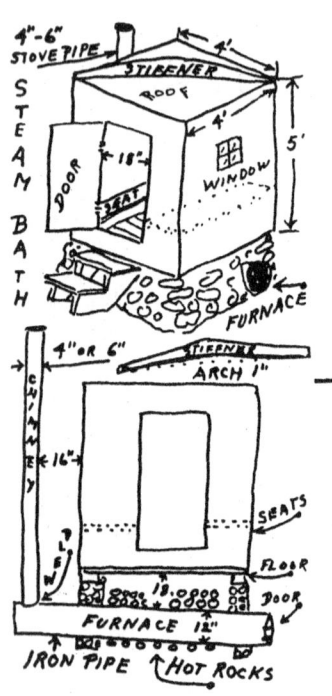

BIG CRACKS IN FLOOR FOR STEAM.
WALLS AND CEILING OF ¼" PLYWOOD, EXTERIOR GLUE LINED INSIDE WITH CELOTEX OR CANE BOARD.
PAINT WITH TRAFFIC LINE PAINT.

"Drink some little time before or after the meal. HL 962.

"Drink taken with meals, water diminishes the flow of the salivary glands; and the colder the water, the greater the injury to the stomach." HL 672.

"Water is the best liquid possible to cleanse the tissues." HL 673.

—BATH

"Twice a week ... take a general bath, as cool as will be agreeable, a little cooler every time, until the skin is toned up." 1T 702.

"Bathe frequently in pure soft water, followed by gentle rubbing." HL 818.

"Upon rising in the morning, most persons would be benefitted by taking a sponge bath, or, if more agreeable, a hand bath, with merely a wash bowl of water; this will remove impurities from the skin." HL 816.

"Frequent bathing is very beneficial, especially at night just before retiring, or upon rising in the morning." HL 817.

"Bathing frees the skin from the accumulation of impurities which are constantly collecting, and keeps the skin moist and supple, thereby increasing and equalizing the circulation." HL 789.

8 LAWS OF HEALTH

—CLOTHES

"If the garments worn are not frequently cleansed from impurities, the pores of the skin absorb again the waste matter thrown off. The impurities of the body, if not allowed to escape, are taken back into the blood and forced upon the internal organs. Nature, to relieve herself of poisonous impurities, makes an effort to free the system, which effort produces fevers and what is termed disease." HL 887.

—FOR PNEUMONIA

—FOMENTATIONS

Wood blanket

Newspaper and rag with hot water

—FOR INFECTION OF HANDS OR FEET

Water + charcoal
    + smart weed
    + mustard

HOT and COLD brings in blood and takes it out. The blood heals
Steam Bath
Take hot soap shower.
Drink 1/2 glass of sea water.
Warm up on vapor bath.
Backs straightened.
Dip in cold water or shower.
More heat in steam room.
Second cold dip.
Third hot steam.
Third cold bath.
Cool off thoroughly then dress.

8 LAWS OF HEALTH

—TUB TREATMENT

(If you have lots of water)
Get in tub, soap off.
Add hot water slowly
Continue to add hot water
When too hot shut off hot water
Add cold water slowly
Letting hot water run out overflow
Stay in cold water till you're chilly
Dry with a rough towel
You will feel great

TO CLEANSE THE BOWELS
DRINK 2 QUARTS
BEFORE BREAKFAST
SPRING WATER 2/3
SEA WATER 1/3

—ENEMA

(Caution too many are habit forming)
For high fevers
Sickness of all kinds
Constipation
For quick relief when sea water cannot be used
Sea water is much better than enemas
Water neither cold nor hot
Drain out all air from hose
Put patient on left side, insert tip, slowly
Turn on water slowly, stop at cramps
Have patient lay on back now
Add water slowly. Gently massage belly.
Give at least 3 cans full, evacuating as necessary.

ENEMA

TODAY DRINK ONE GALLON PURE SOFT WATER

AFTER SEA WATER DRINK USE THIS AND YOU WILL RECOVER.

—DRINK

Pure water to drink and fresh air to breathe invigorate the vital organs, purify the blood, and help nature in her task of overcoming the bad conditions of the system. HL 786.

8 LAWS OF HEALTH

—FEVERS

Nature, to relieve herself of poisonous impurities, makes an effort to free the system, which effort produces fevers and what is termed disease. But even then, if those who are afflicted would assist nature in her efforts by the use of pure, soft water, much suffering would be prevented. HL 977.

—SALLOW SKIN

Their sallow skins indicate that they are bilious. Observe regular habits of rising early, eat sparingly, thus relieving the system of unnecessary burden, and encourage cheerfulness. Take proper exercise in the open air, bathe frequently, and drink freely of pure, soft water. HL 964.

GOD

TRUST IN DIVINE POWER

Take your troubles to God in prayer. Jesus will forgive your sins if you ask Him. "If we confess our sins, He is faithful and just to forgive us our sins, and to cleanse us from all unrighteousness." 1 John 1:9.

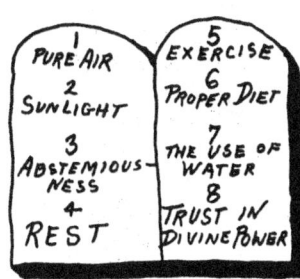

"If any of you lack wisdom, let him ask of God, that giveth to all men liberally, and upbraideth not; and it shall be given him." James 1:5.

8 LAWS OF HEALTH

"Is any sick among you.... The prayer of faith shall save the sick." James 5:14-20.

"It is labor lost to teach people to go to God as a healer of their infirmities, unless they are educated also to lay aside every wrong practice." HL 1015.

"Many have expected that God would keep them from sickness merely because they have asked Him to do so. But God did not regard their prayers because their faith was not made perfect by works. God will not work a miracle to keep those from sickness who have no care for themselves. But are continually violating the laws of health, and make no effort to prevent disease. When we do all we can on our part to have health, then we may expect that the blessed results will follow."

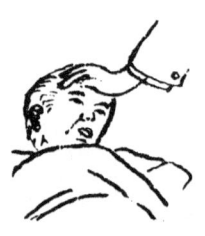

"If we regard iniquity in our hearts, the Lord will not hear us." Ps. 66:18.

"God will not work a miracle to change natural causes which you can control." HL 1026.

"God is just as willing to restore the sick to health now.

8 LAWS OF HEALTH

Christ is the same compassionate physician now that He was during His earthly ministry. In Him there is healing balm for every disease, restoring power for every infirmity. His disciples in this time are to pray for the sick as verily as the disciples of old prayed. And recoveries will follow; for 'The prayer of faith shall save the sick.' We have the Holy Spirit's power, the calm assurance of faith, that can claim God's promises." MH 225-7.

" 'They shall lay hands on the sick, and they shall recover,' is just as trustworthy now as in the days of the Apostles." MH 226.

"And God hears prayer. Christ has said, 'If ye shall ask anything in My Name, I will do it.' Again, He says, 'If any man serve Me, ... Him will My Father honor.' If we live according to His word, every precious promise He has given will be fulfilled to us." MH 226-7.

PRAYER FOR THE SICK

"Where the way is clear for the offering up of prayer for the sick, the case should be committed to the Lord in calm faith, not with a storm of excitement. He alone is acquainted with the past life of the individual and knows what his future will be.

8
TRUST in
DIVINE POWER

8 LAWS OF HEALTH

"All that we are required to do is to ask God to raise up the sick if in accordance with His will, believing that He hears the reasons which we present, and the fervent prayers offered. If the Lord sees that it will best honor Him, He will answer our prayers. But to urge recovery without submission to His will, is not right.... In perfect confidence rest the matter in His hands. If the life of the sick can glorify Him, we pray that they may live; nevertheless, not as we will, but as He wills. Our faith can be just as firm, and more reliable, by committing the desire to the all wise God, and without feverish anxiety, in perfect confidence, trusting all to Him. Our petitions must not take the form of a command, but of intercession for Him to do the thing we desire of Him." HL 1028

APPENDICITIS

SYMPTOMS: Abdominal pain, usually severe and generally throughout the abdomen. Nausea and vomiting. Localization of pain in right lower of abdomen. Fever 99 to 101 f.

CAUSE: Meat eating, breaking 8 laws of health. Constipation.

TREATMENT:

1. Give 4 tablespoonsful of olive oil to drink.
2. Apply cold lemon juice compress to area.
3. Or cold epsom salts to abdomen.
4. Give gently several enemas.
5. Follow carefully the 8 laws of health.

ASTHMA

SYMPTOMS: Coughing, wheezing, hard breathing.

CAUSE: Constipation, sour stomach, nerves, breaking the laws of health.

TREATMENT: Follow carefully the 8 laws of health. Cleanse the bowels with the sea water treatment.

HERBS: Lobelia seed tea. 13 hour treatment take no food upon arising in the morning. Take a tea of boneset herb and cayenne pepper every 1/2 hour 3 times, then strong peppermint tea with a little lobelia tea every 1/2 hour. More lobelia and less peppermint each time. Vomit often, if need be. About the 10 to 13 hour long strings of heavy mucus are spit up.

A

THIS IS A VERY ROUGH TREATMENT BUT NOT DANGEROUS. TREATMENT MUST BE GIVEN BY ANOTHER PERSON WHO FOLLOWS INSTRUCTIONS CAREFULLY.

Now take less and less lobelia and more and more peppermint. Conclude at any time now that the heavy mucous is all out. 14 hours treatment generally does a complete job of asthma with no bad effects and they are a new person the next day.

ATHLETE'S FOOT

KEEP FEET DRY IN BETWEEN THE TOES. WASH WITH STRONG SOAP OFTEN. KEEP SOCKS CLEAN.

1. Wormwood tea applied to skin.

2. Rub on banana skin.

3. Pound up avocado seed, apply to skin

4. Creosote bush tea.

AMOEBA (AMOEBIC DYSENTERY)

SYMPTOMS: Diarrhea, cramps. Stools have pus, blood, and mucous. 20 or more bowel movements a day.

CAUSE: Infected from human manure by careless handling of food by infected persons. Gardens raised with human excretion or manure.

REMEDY: Pulverized charcoal, put water upon it and give this water to the sick to drink putting bandages of the charcoal over the bowels and stomach.

Also charcoal and olive oil (or any vegetable salad oil) stir and add a little natural salt. Eat a big spoonful every 1/2 hour. This takes care of all kinds of dysentery.

APOPLEXY (STROKE)

CAUSE: Your health is greatly injured by overeating and eating at improper times. This causes a determination of the blood to the brain and you are in danger of apoplexy; and if you continue to disobey the laws of health, your life will be cut short suddenly. HL 957.

SYMPTOMS: The patient falls suddenly as a small blood vessel breaks in the brain. Sudden paralysis of one side of the body and 1/2 of face.

TREATMENT: Apply ice water cloth to head. Loosen clothes around neck. Keep head raised. Warm hands and feet. Continue cold to head for 7 days. Keep extremities warm. Keep bowels open daily. See that bladder empties 3 times daily.

HERBS: Cayenne pepper in a little water.

The next stroke may be your last.

ARTHRITIS

SYMPTOMS: Pain in the joints; slight tenderness on pressure; more or less swelling of joints. Pain increased at night, and by bad weather.

CAUSE: Sugar, salt, white flour and all refined foods with meat, tobacco, alcohol and eating in between meals. Check your 8 laws of health.

TREATMENT: Stop the causes. Italian treatment, rough but very effective. Crush garlic, spread in cloth like butter on bread. Wrap poultice around arthritic joint 2 to 12 hours,

B

WORRY AND MILK ARE TWO COMMON CAUSES OF ARTHRITIS.

CREOSOTE BUSH IS SOLD UNDER THE NAME OF CHAPARRAL TEA.

which will raise a large burn blister full of water. This will break and run out drawing the disease out of joint. Now heal up the burn with Aloe Vera inside juice, and see amazing results in a few days.

HERBS: Creosote bush leaf tea. Drink lots of it. Avocado seed, pound, make strong tea apply to skin. Mandrake tea drink 3 cups daily.

B

BABIES

Don't cover their heads while sleeping. Keep the babies arms and legs warm. Give the lungs fresh air to breathe. Feeding at any and all hours is very bad. Feed not closer than 4 hours. 5 hours between feedings is best. Give only water in between meals. There is nothing impure in clean sand and dry earth. Emanations from the body defile and require washing. Baby clothes should not be too tight.

Tobacco using parents poison baby.

Stomach upset give peppermint tea.

Milk: Mama's best. Goat milk next best.

Ripe banana and ripe coconut ground and squeezed very good.

COWS MUST BE HEALTHY.

—MILK BOTTLE

MILK MUST NOT BE PASTEURIZED.

GET A NEW ONE THAT DON'T DRIP.

If the milk drips from the nipple when turned down the hole is too large, this will give the baby indigestion. The hole in the bottle nipple should be very small. Make the baby chew his milk and take it slowly.

—BELLY ACHE

SYMPTOMS: Vomiting, purging, collapse, very thirsty, temperature 105-108 degrees, pulse rapid, feeble urine scanty.

CAUSE: Mostly caused by feeding too much and too often. Also improper baby food.

TREATMENT: Stop all food for one or two days. Give 1/3 sea water with 2/3 fresh warm water to cleanse the bowels first thing in the morning or 3 enemas. *Followed by plenty of pure fresh water to drink* (warm in cool weather). Charcoal water strained. Peppermint leaf tea. Start feeding fruit juice. Keep a full 5 hours in between meals. No food or drink water only in between meals.

BEE STINGS

SEE: Insect Stings

Pull out the stinger if still in. Quick apply mud. Mud and charcoal still better.

BELLY ACHE

Take charcoal. Drink warm salty water to clear stomach up or down. Take charcoal every 1/2 hour.

BITES OF INSECTS ETC.

"Snake bites and the sting of reptiles and poisonous insects could often be rendered harmless by the use of charcoal poultices." P.of H. 26.

Mud and charcoal reduce swelling and take away pain.

B

BLEEDING INTERNALLY OR EXTERNALLY

Cayenne pepper, drink it in a little water or in a wound. It equalizes circulation, stops bleeding and relieves shock. Open wounds use soft pine pitch or balsam.

BLACK EYE

A bruise—a charcoal poultice in a bag, or lemon juice poultice.

BLACK WIDOW SPIDER BITE

SYMPTOMS: A sharp pain. Spot swells and reddens. Dizzy feeling, sea legs, cramps in abdomen, children go into fits or have hard breathing.

TREATMENT: Apply suction to get out as much poison as possible. Give cayenne pepper in a little water to equalize the circulation and keep the heart going. Mud poultice, or mud and charcoal poultice.

BLADDER TROUBLES

Corn silk tea in large quantities and often. Shave grass is also good if you don't have corn silk.

BLIND SPOTS

Dark spots appear to be floating in front of the eyes. Cleanse the liver by obeying the 8 laws of health. Stop meat eating.

B

BLOOD PRESSURE

HIGH BLOOD PRESSURE: Overweight ruddy complexion, ringing in ears, throbbing of the head.

Eat nothing in between meals.

Stop all meats. Eat a good breakfast at 6:00 a.m. eat a good meal at 12 noon. Eat nothing more that day. This program will reduce the overweight and unclog the overworked liver. The eating of garlic also helps to reduce high blood pressure. Worry is often the cause of high blood pressure.

LOW BLOOD PRESSURE: Lack of energy, headache, shortness of breath, dizziness, etc.

CAUSES: Impoverished diet, constipation, anemia, bad teeth.

TREATMENT: Cleanse bowels with sea water. Obey laws of health.

BLOOD POISON

SYMPTOMS: A generalized infection around a wound, looks red and angry.

CAUSE: Infection

TREATMENT: Quick with hot and cold to the infected part. Continue every little while till red streaks disappear.

HERBS: Turpentine, pine pitch, balsam, cayenne pepper, golden seal, charcoal poultice.

B

FIGS

2 KINGS 20:7 "TAKE A LUMP OF FIGS..... AND LAID IT ON THE BOIL, AND HE RECOVERED.

RED AND SORE — PUSS — BOIL

BOILS

SYMPTOMS: Painful, but limited infection, with a single core, or a mass of boils called a carbuncle.

CAUSE: Nature unloading poisons from the body. Constipation, refined foods, drugs.

TREATMENT: Do not pinch or squeeze as it may spread infection. Apply ice. Hot and cold brings it to a head quicker. Wet bandage of common salt in water is good.

BRAIN

—STUDENT

"The student sits day after day in a close room, bending over his desk or table, his chest contracted, his lungs crowded. His brain is taxed to the utmost, while his body is inactive. He cannot take full, deep inspirations; his blood moves sluggishly; his feet are cold, his head hot.... Let them take regular exercise that will cause them to breathe deep and full, and they will soon feel that they have a new hold on life." HL 589.

—SEX EXCESS

"Sexual excess will take from the brain the substance needed to nourish the system, and will most effectively exhaust the vitality." SA 48.

Wrong habits of eating, dressing or sleeping affect the brain. HL 834.

B

Morning exercise, in walking in the free invigorating air of heaven ... is the surest safeguard against congestions of the brain. HL 574.

LOW BLOOD PRESSURE:INSANE

Thousands are today in insane asylums whose minds became unbalanced by novel reading. HL 842.

—BENUMBED

The brain nerve energy is benumbed and almost paralyzed by overeating. HL 689.

—CONCUSSION

SYMPTOMS: Unconsciousness, temporary or prolonged; sometimes walking and talking after an accident, yet completely unconscious. Eyes unequal pupils, dizziness.

FIRST AID TREATMENT: Keep patient quietly lying down. Do not give stimulants. Cool applications to head and neck are soothing. Encourage person if conscious. Apply heat to hands and feet if cold. Dark room best. Moving should be delayed for some time. Keep warm.

UNEQUAL IS A BUMP ON THE HEAD.

1. Prayer to God.
2. A very gentle use of water.
3. A very spare diet till the danger of fever is past.
4. Well-ventilated rooms day and night.
5. Do not take one grain of medicine. (2T 18)

BUT DON'T CHILL KEEP HANDS AND FEET WARM.

B

BRUISES:

Injury to which skin is discolored but not broken.

TREATMENT: Bruises—hands, etc. "Pulverized charcoal in a bag and used in fomentations.... If wet in smart weed, boiled, it is still better." P of H 24.

HERBS: Lemon juice

BREAST CANCER

SEE: Cancer

BUNION

Inflammation and thickening of the joint of the big toe, on the ball of the foot at the base of the big toe.

CAUSE: The big toe is displaced, and forced in the direction of the little toe.

TREATMENT: Get 2 sizes wider and 2 sizes longer shoes. Better yet go barefoot. Put something in between big toe to push it back straight again.

BURNS

CAUSE: Exposure to heat, chemicals, sunshine, electricity.

TREATMENT:

1. Ice or ice water quick will positively prevent blistering.
2. Keep in cold water and ice till all fire is out of burn.
3. Shock, give cayenne pepper or strong peppermint tea. Keep head low, warm with blankets.

4. Place part or patient in a bathtub of ocean water and slowly cut off clothes as not to disturb any skin in bad burns. Keep in ocean water (warm) for 3 weeks, night and day.

For 3rd degree burns. While you are getting ocean water use plain water with 2 pounds of table salt to the tubful. This will save a life when nothing else will.

SEA WATER

5. Charcoal poultice is very good

6. Mashed onion poultice extracts the fire and relieves the pain.

7. Kerosene is what blacksmiths use for burns.

8. Mashed raw potatoes is very good.

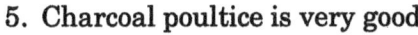

CANCERS—SKIN, STOMACH, BLOOD, GLANDS, BREAST, LIP

SYMPTOMS: SKIN cancers are most common on the exposed portion of face and hands. An open sore that refuses to heal or a dark blotch that slowly spreads.

CAUSE: Burns from glasses, Sunburn, old scars, shaving soap, meat-eating, and pork-eating. Breaking the laws of health.

TREATMENT: Wood sorrel or sheep sorrel, fresh. Rub leaves in hand to a juicy pulp. Apply as poultice into cancer. Tape it on. Don't use band aide. Change twice daily.

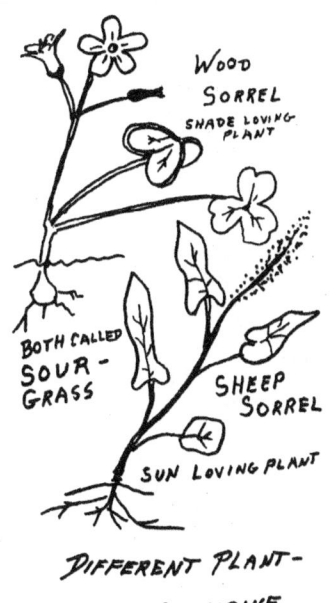

DIFFERENT PLANT—
SAME MEDICINE

C

—PORK

The eating of pork has produced scrofula, leprosy and cancerous tumors. Pork-eating is still causing the most intense suffering to the human race. Diseases and its Causes, p. 14.

Cancers, tumors, and inflammatory diseases are largely caused by meat eating. HL 765.

—STOMACH

SYMPTOMS: Pain at the pit of the stomach of a burning or gnawing character, increased by food; tenderness on pressure over the stomach. Nausea and frequently vomiting. The vomited matters often resembling coffee grounds. Hard pulsating tumor felt near the pit of the stomach. Great loss of weight, yellow complexion, great exhaustion, swelling ankles.

CAUSE: Meat eating, pork, grease, lard, butter, tea, coffee, tobacco, alcohol, sugar, eating in between meals, breaking the 8 laws of health.

TREATMENT: stop all bad habits, check very carefully the 8 laws of health. Stop eating all meat, milk, eggs, butter, cheese. Stop using all cooked, processed or preserved foods or anything that has been heated. Eat only raw ripe fruits, grains (sprouted) nuts (not too many), vegetables as near as God and nature has made them. Keep a full 6 hours between your meals. EAT some sea weeds daily. Drink a little sea water daily.

C

HERBS: Creosote bush leaves tea, strong, with a little honey. Drink lots of it. It is very bitter. An angel gave this remedy to a dying man in a dream and he got well. It works.

CREOSOTE BUSH MISCALLED CHAPARRAL TEA.

Aloe Vera. Use the inside of the leaf only. Add 1 cup of juice to 1 quart of water and beat it up. Drink 2 quarts of this mixture daily. Rub fresh pulp and juice all over the skin from head to toe. Also an injection of a small enema retained of the aloe vera juice and water one quart daily. Where lumps of cancer are near the skin apply a poultice of figs. (2 Kings 20:7) This works wonders.

CREOSOTE BUSH OR CHAPARRAL. EACH LEAF IS DOUBLE. GROWS IN HOT DRY LAND. THE ABOVE IS ABOUT NATURAL SIZE.

PAIN: Greatly reduced by a poultice of charcoal and mud. Linseed oil stops pain in cancer. Also other oils as sunflower, sesame and soy bean oil.

Cancers, tumors, and inflammatory diseases are largely caused by meat eating. Pork has produced leprosy and cancerous tumors.

CATARACT

Opacity of eye lens. Follow the 8 laws of health. Cleanse the body. Massage the eye by gentle cupping massage with a suction cup. Cataracts often cleared in a few weeks.

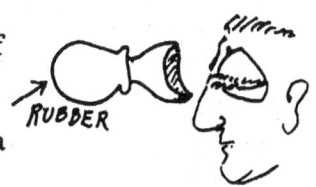

RUBBER

EATING TOO MUCH FRUIT AND NOT ENOUGH GREEN LEAF FOODS.

CANKER IN THE MOUTH

SYMPTOMS: White spots on mucous membrane of the mouth and tongue. Chewing is painful.

CAUSES: Digestive disturbances, bad food, bad air, use of mercury medicines.

C

TREATMENT: Go on a diet of raw food for a few days.

HERBS: Red raspberry leaf tea. Golden seal root.

CHEESE

The effect of cheese is deleterious. Cheese should never be introduced into the stomach. HL 425.

CHICKEN POX

SYMPTOMS: Slight fever and skin eruption

INCUBATION: 8 to 18 days. Makes its appearance in crops and passes through successive stages of macules, papules, vesicles, and crusts. Slight fever and eruption of short duration. No complications.

CAUSE: A disease of childhood; usually only one attack. The body getting rid of poisons in the system caused by disobedience to God's 8 laws of health.

TREATMENT: Rest in bed, fresh air, cleanse the bowels, drink freely of pure water hot or cold.

CHILDREN: EAT ALL HOURS

Children are permitted to indulge their tastes freely to eat at all hours. The digestive organs like a mill which is continually kept running become enfeebled, vital force is called from the brain to aid the stomach in its overwork, and thus the mental powers are weakened. The unnatural stimulation and wear of the vital forces make the children nervous, impatient of restraint, self willed and irritable. HL 49.

C

—CLOTHES

Parents who dress their children with their extremities naked, or nearly so, are sacrificing the life and health of their children to fashion. HL 773.

—MEALS

They (children) should be allowed only plain food, of that quality that would preserve to them the best condition of health and that should be partaken of only at regular periods, not oftener than three times a day, and two meals would be better than three. HL 627.

—EDUCATION

During the first 6 or 7 years of a child's life special attention should be given to its physical training rather than the intellect.—SA 83.

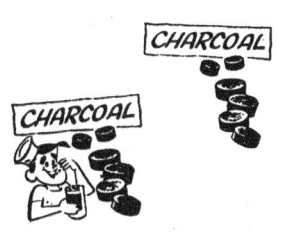

CHOLERA, ASIATIC

SYMPTOMS: Incubation period from a few hours to 4 or 5 days. The disease usually begins suddenly, often with severe cramps in the back or in the legs and the arms. It may begin with diarrhea and colicky pains. Shortly after the onset the stools become thin, and contain small, white, curd-like masses. Severe vomiting at the onset. Great thirst, urine diminishes, skin dries up, skin feels cold, lips, face and the fingernails become bluish. Fever slight. Not contagious.

CAUSE: Contaminated water, food.

C

TREATMENT: Eat charcoal and drink charcoal water. Give cayenne pepper. Give sea water cleansing.

CIRCULATION

Perfect health depends upon perfect circulation. HL 737.

COLDS

SYMPTOMS: A dry, scratchy, irritated feeling in the nose or the back of the throat is usually the first sign of a cold. Chilly sensations, feeling of fatigue, deafness, hoarse, red nose, damp eyes, stuffy nose, sneezing, coughing.

CAUSE: A cold is caused by eating between meals, at all hours and overloading the stomach and liver. Eating candy, ice cream, pop, cake, grease foods, staying up late at night, not enough clothes on the arms and legs. Sleeping rooms windows closed. Over work. Not enough fresh air. Staying indoors too much.

Eating white flour products, sugar, clog the system. All these things fill the system with mucous toxins which the cold (an effort of nature) is trying to clean out of your body while you are putting in the filth. A cold is a friend trying to save your life.

TREATMENT: Stop breaking God's laws of health. Stop eating for awhile. Help nature get rid of mucous poisons by drinking lots of warm water.

Cleanse the bowels by drinking a lot of 1/3 sea water with 2/3 hot water. 2 qts. for an adult.

Breathe fresh air day and night. Sweat by sauna bath, or hot bath in tub increasing the heat as hot as bearable then add cold water slowly till cold.

—SAFE-GUARD AGAINST

Morning exercise, in walking in the free invigorating air of heaven, is the surest safe-guard against colds, coughs, congestions of the brain and lungs, and a hundred other diseases. HL 903.

HERBS: Sore throat—cayenne pepper.

To increase sweating—blue vervain tea.

For chest colds—smartweed boiled in water used in fomentations.

Cough—Horehound tea.

Fevers—Sage tea.

COFFEE: TOUCH NOT

Tea has an influence to excite the nerves, and coffee benumbs the brain; both are highly injurious. HL 487

By the use of tea and coffee an appetite is formed for tobacco, and this encourages the appetite for liquors. HL 504.

The only safe course is to touch not, taste not, handle not... tea, coffee, wines, tobacco, opium, and alcoholic drinks. HL 505.

C

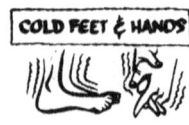

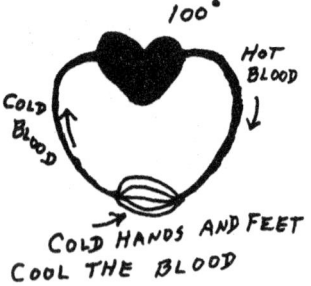

COLD HANDS—FEET

The extremities are chilled, and the heart has thrown upon it double labor, to force the blood into these chilled extremities; and when the blood has performed its circuit through the body, and return to the heart, it is not the same vigorous, warm current which left it. It has been chilled in its passage through the limbs. The heart weakened by too great labor and poor circulation of poor blood, is then compelled to still greater exertion, to throw the blood to the extremities which are never as healthfully warm as other parts of the body. The heart fails in its efforts, and the limbs become habitually cold, and the blood, which is chilled away from the extremities, is thrown back upon the lungs and brain. HL 550.

COLD—WOMEN

There is but one woman in a thousand who clothes her limbs as she should. Women should clothe their limbs as thoroughly as do men. HL 548.

—CHILDREN IN COLD CLIMATES

Parents who dress their children with their extremities naked, or nearly so, are sacrificing the life and health of their children to fashion. HL 773.

CONGESTION—NAKED LIMBS

Their limbs, as well as their arms, are left almost naked.... The heart, weakened by too great labor, fails in its efforts, and the limbs become habitually cold and the blood which is chilled away from the extremities, is thrown back upon the lungs and brain, and inflammation and congestion of the lungs or the brain is the result. HL 850.

CONSUMPTION—CLOTHES (tuberculosis)

Many who have died of consumption might have lived their allotted term of life had they dressed in accordance with the laws of their being. HL 726.

SYMPTOMS: Debility, loss of flesh and strength; fever 102 to 104 degrees irregular; cough, hurried breathing, a brown fissured tongue; weak rapid pulse; enlarged spleen. Afternoon fever night sweats; spitting blood.

CAUSE: Excesses, naked arms and legs, poor food, overwork, lack of exercise, loss of sleep, sexual excesses, masturbation, no fresh air, meat.

TREATMENT: Keep arms and legs warm; stop eating in between meals. Get 23 hours of fresh air a day. Take sunbaths. Take sea water every morning 1/3-2/3 to build up the blood and to keep the bowels clean. 6 vegetables, 2 fruits, one fat, one sweet food, all natural.

HERBS: Strong yerba Santa leaf tea

CONSTIPATION

SYMPTOMS: Inability to have a bowel movement. Three meals a day should have three evacuations a day.

C

Eat natural foods unsprayed with the peeling and small seeds. Swallow cherry seeds, water melon seeds, grape skins and seeds. You don't need to chew them, but it is alright if you do. They will not grow out of your ears or nose, but they will help get the bowels moving normally.

Get shoes to fit the foot shape. Don't cramp toes. It ruins the nerves.

Less than this is constipation. Weariness, headache, bad taste in the mouth.

CAUSE: Soft refined food, worry, anxiety, fear, lack of water drinking, lack of roughage in diet. Lack of physical exercise.

TREATMENT: Stop eating or drinking anything except water in between meals. Have a full 5 or 6 hours between meals. Eat roughage as grape skins and seeds, water melon seeds whole or chew them. Apple skins. Raw uncooked fruit and vegetables, (not at the same meal) Take sea water warm 1/3 sea water to 2/3 fresh water, 3 to 10 glass fulls before breakfast.

Enemas can be used in emergencies but too many of them become habit forming. Don't get the enema habit.

CORNS AND CALLOUSES

SYMPTOMS: Horny thickening of the skin.

CAUSE: Pressure or friction. Shoes too short or too narrow.

REMEDY: Get shoes 2 sizes longer and 2 sizes wider than the ones you are now wearing. Better yet, go bare foot or wear sandals.

COUGH

When the extremities are not properly clad, the blood is driven to the head ... fullness about the chest producing cough or palpitation of the heart, on account of too much blood in that locality. HL 552.

Naked extremities.... Circulation not equalized.... There is a sense of fullness about the chest; producing cough. HL 773.

Walking in the free invigorating air of heaven ... is the surest safeguard against colds, coughs, etc. HL 731.

CROUP

SEE: Diphtheria (Kerosene, a few drops in throat)

A childhood disease, commonest at the ages of two and three.

Age 3 months to 8 years.

SYMPTOMS: Harsh, hoarse, croaking-croupy cough and labored breathing. Usually comes on suddenly at night and is not accompanied by fever.

EMERGENCY TREATMENT: Warm moist air.

CAUSE: Eating between meals, overeating, wrong kinds of foods, sour stomach. Meals too close together, indigestion, constipation, candy, ice cream, sugars, etc.

TREATMENT: Enema, ocean water, cold water or ice applied to neck. 8 laws of health.

HERBS: Onion juice. Teaspoonful every 15 min. Hot foot bath with cayenne, smart weed or mustard in the foot bath.

CROUP (babies)

Turpentine 1/3 and 2/3 water. Apply to throat and chest as hot as can be borne every few moments. It quickly opens the breathing tubes safely.

D

CUTS

Balsam, or the clear pitch of the pine or fir trees, is the best to put in cuts, wounds or nail puncture. A most powerful healer inside or out.

As a second best turpentine is very good, but keep off all bandages when you use turpentine for if covered it will blister the skin.

Cayenne pepper will stop bleeding. Golden seal, or the green juice of any edible plant will stop infection and blood poison.

CYSTITIS

SYMPTOMS: Inflammation of the bladder, difficulties or abnormalities in passing urine, as frequency, urgency and pain or obstruction. (Hot and Cold Sitz Bath)

CAUSE: Going too long without emptying the bladder. Drugs produce it. Too much acid foods and not enough green leaf foods. Not enough drinking water.

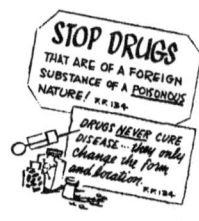

TREATMENT: Corn silk tea 3 times daily, not and cold sitz bath. Drink a lot of lemon water. Cleanse the bowels. Obey the 8 laws of health.

DEAFNESS

SYMPTOMS: Loss of hearing partial or complete.

CAUSE: Quinine, ringing noises in ears. Wax in ears. Foreign bodies in ears cause explosive noises. Over-taxation. Over work.

TREATMENT: Onion juice, 5 to 10 drops in ear several times a day. Have wax removed. Cleanse bowels and skin. Almond oil is good. Olive oil. Wintergreen oil. Obey 8 laws of health.

DIABETES

SYMPTOMS: Increased thirst. Abnormal discharge of urine, susceptible to infection. Urine pale and watery. Gangrene sets in an injury easily. Weakness and drowsiness. Abnormal amounts of sugar in the urine and blood.

CAUSE: Faulty nutrition. Wrong diet. Wrong eating and drinking habits, sugars, fats and starches, denatured food, white flour, tobacco, soft drinks, tea, coffee, sodas, baking powder, hard grease, butter, flesh meat, worry.

TREATMENT: Take 3 cups of soy bean coffee daily. (Take soy beans, roast them in the oven till nice and brown. Coarse grind and use for coffee). This will often heal up the condition in a week or two.

HERBS: Corn silk tea. Raw Jerusalem artichoke.

DIARRHEA

SEE: Amoeba

SYMPTOMS: Loose bowels; frequent or excessive bowel movements.

CAUSE: Food poisoning. Ptomaine poisoning, nature cleaning house.

D

TREATMENT: Sea water cleansing of 1/3 fresh water, warm, 8 to 10 glasses. Then give 6 charcoal tablets every hour. Drink lots of water.

DIPHTHERIA

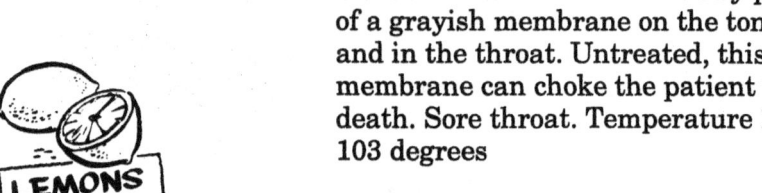

SYMPTOMS: Characterized by patches of a grayish membrane on the tonsils and in the throat. Untreated, this membrane can choke the patient to death. Sore throat. Temperature 100 to 103 degrees

CAUSE: Direct contact with a human carrier or their articles. Incubation 2 to 8 days. Lack of fresh air, living indoors too much. Breaking the 8 laws of health.

TREATMENT: Gargle with a little kerosene. Sip pineapple juice. Child give a few drops of kerosene according to age. Cleanse the bowels. Hot and cold to throat and chest. Sip lemon juice Cayenne in/out. Follow 8 laws of health.

DROPSY

SYMPTOMS: Swelling of feet, legs, abdomen, by water collecting also of lung cavity or even in brain. Scrotum dropsy (testicles fill with water) worse in evening. Signs of heart disease, anemia, kidney trouble.

CAUSE: Disobedience to the 8 laws of health.

TREATMENT: Daily enema, sweat baths, stop all tea, coffee, tobacco, alcohol and animal products. Eat fruit, grains, nuts, vegetables. USE NO SALT.

D

A poultice of cabbage leaves pounded is very helpful. Also a poultice of cayenne pepper is very good.
HERBS: Corn Silk tea. Aloe boiled with wormwood tea drives out water. Drink vervain tea, produces sweating. Elder root bark tea.

DOG BITE
SEE: Hydrophobia

DROWNING:
1. Loosen clothes quickly.
2. Turn body face down. Put your arms under his belly and try to lift him. This drains water from wind pipe for 1/2 minute.
3. Face down, head turned to side, see that tongue is forward. Nose and mouth open.
4. Start artificial respiration quickly as every second counts. Press on lower ribs and release about 12 times a minute. DON'T STOP.
5. Keep patient warm with blanket or clothes.
6. Don't give up too soon. Keep going for hours.
7. Pray to God.

DRUGS
"Whatever they may be, derange the nervous system." HL 865.
"Everywhere you go you will see deformity, disease, and imbecility, which in very many cases can be traced directly back to drug poisons." HL 1051.
"There are more who die from the use of drugs than all who would have died of disease had nature been left to do her own work." HL 1045.

73

D

DONT USE
THESE POISONOUS HERBS

Henbane Leaves
Jimson Weed
Juniper Leaves
Lily of the Valley Leaves
Lily of the Valley Root
May Lily Leaves
May Lily Root
Nux Vomica

Pennyroyal
Rue Leaves
Savin Tops
Squaw Mint
Stramonium Leaves
Tansy Herb
Yellow Jessamine

Aconite Root
Belladonna Leaves
Cotton Root Bark
Digitalis Leaves
Ergot
Foxglove Leaves
Gelsemium Root
Hellebore Root

"Drugging should be forever abandoned; for while it does not cure any malady, it enfeebles the system, making it more susceptible to disease." HL 1044.

DRUGS

"Drugs never cure disease, they only change its form and location. When drugs are introduced into the system, for a time they seem to have a beneficial effect. A change may take place, but the disease is not cured. It will manifest itself in some other form. The disease which the drug was given to cure may disappear, but only to reappear in a new form, such as skin diseases, ulcers, painful diseased joints, and sometimes a more dangerous and deadly form. Nature keeps struggling and the patient suffers with different ailments, ... and death follows." HL 1040

DRUGS

"Lives have been lost which might have been saved if drugs had not been resorted to." HL 1056.

"Every poisonous preparation in the vegetable and mineral kingdoms, taken into the system, will leave its wretched influence, affecting the liver and lungs." HL 730.

DRUGS—DISCARD

"Discard all drugs, and live simply, without using tea, coffee, liquor, or spices." P of H 15.

DRUG ADDICTION—STOP

1. STOP ALL DRUGS
2. USE ICE ON WITHDRAWAL CRAMP PAINS
3. HERBS: Lobelia tea. Cayenne pepper.

PRAY TO GOD. THERE IS A REAL GOD IN HEAVEN THAT WILL HELP IF YOU WILL CONFESS YOUR SINS AND ASK HIM.

DYSENTERY

SYMPTOMS: Fever, great thirst, urine scanty, tongue red, pain in the abdomen, diarrhea, cramps sometimes bloody or mucous-filled stools, ten to twenty bowel movements daily.

CAUSE: Some form of contaminated food or water.

TREATMENT: Pulverize charcoal, put water upon it and give this water to the sick to drink. Eat charcoal every 1/2 hour. Put bandages of charcoal over the bowels and stomach.

E

EARACHE

SYMPTOMS: Ear becomes red or swollen, pain, sensation of fullness, ringing in the ears, he may have earache.

CAUSE: Dirty bowels, dirty blood, refined foods, sugar. Breaking the laws of health.

TREATMENT: Cleanse the bowels with sea water or enema. Hot food bath. Apply heat by hot salt in a bag. Apply heat by hot salt in a bag. Drop 5 drops of onion juice in ear. Lemon juice in oil a few drops is good in ear. Almond oil or peach seed oil is good. Baked onion poultice when pain is severe.

E

EAT—TOO MUCH

Nearly all the members of the human family eat more than the system requires. If more food, even of a simple quality, is placed in the stomach than the living machinery requires, this surplus becomes a burden. HL 400.

—LESS

The stomach becomes weary by being kept constantly at work; the remedy such require is to eat less frequently and less liberally, and be satisfied with plain simple food, eating twice, or at the most three times a day. HL 695.

—3RD MEAL

"If the third meal be eaten at all, it should be light, and several hours before going to bed." HL 385.

—BETWEEN MEALS

"You should never let a morsel pass your lips between your regular meals." HL 392.

—PORK

"The eating of pork has produced scrofula, leprosy, and cancerous humors. Pork-eating is still causing the most intense suffering to the human race." Disease and its Causes 14.

—MEAT

"Cancers, tumors, and pulmonary diseases are largely caused by meat eating." CH 133.

E

EDEMA

SEE: Dropsy

Collection of water in tissue.

ELECTRIC SHOCK

Remove from current. Careful you don't get it. Open mouth and remove false teeth which may get in the way of breathing. Pull tongue forward in mouth as the tongue is often swallowed causing them to get no air. Give artificial respiration hours after it looks hopeless. Don't stop. Work pray.

DON'T GIVE UP FOR HOURS.

ENEMA

The use of water to clean out the lower bowels by a bucket and small hose with a small smooth tip inserted in the rectum.

Lay person on left side. Container filled with luke warm water. Drain out all air. Lubricate enema tip with oil, vaseline or wet with water. Insert tip 1/2 inch turn on the water. Slowly insert tip following water. Give slowly. Turn patient on back with knees bent up. Slowly let water massaging belly. Then a good evacuation will follow. Repeat 3 times in a row, higher each time. Don't get the enema habit. Use sea water cleansing it is much better.

GIVE AT LEAST 3 FULL CANS FULL OF WATER. GO SLOW 1/2 HOUR EACH

LET IN ONE SPOON-FULL AT A TIME BY PINCHING HOSE

POCKETS IN COLON NEED TO BE CAREFULLY CLEANED.

SEA WATER CLEANSING IS THE BEST.

EAT SEEDS, YOU NEED THEM TO SCRAPE OUT.

EPILEPSY—CAUSE CONSTIPATION

SYMPTOMS: The patient falls during the attack, often injuring himself, frothing at mouth. He may bite his tongue, pass urine, and awake to realize

E

SEA WATER IS BETTER THAN SALT.

something has happened. Place pad between teeth during attack to prevent biting tongue.

CAUSE: Brain injury, alcoholism, retention of urine in blood stream, improper diet, tobacco, sexual excesses, self-abuse, tea, coffee, in short breaking the laws of health in some way.

TREATMENT: Relieve constipation. Eat only fresh fruit, grains sprouted, nuts and vegetables. Follow the 8 laws of health. Take sun baths and sweat baths. Eat roughage as apple skins, water melon seeds. Take sea water mix for constipation.

ECZEMA

SYMPTOMS: Rough, red skin rashes that come in patches. May or may not itch or burn. May be swollen, blistered, scaly, or oozing.

CAUSE: The skin is throwing poison out from the body caused by breaking the laws of health. Malnutrition.

TREATMENT: Cleanse the body and build health with sea water mix 1/3 sea water and 2/3 fresh warm water, 3 days in a row each week. Drink all you can before breakfast. Obey the 8 laws of health. Rub sea water on the skin all over. Eat sea weed.

EYES—PAIN, WEAK, INFLAMMATION

"Soft flannel cloths wet in Hot water and salt, will bring relief quickly.' p.of H. 4.

"The more severe inflammation of the eyes will be relieved by a poultice of charcoal. Put in a big and dipped in hot or cold water as will best suit the case. P of H 10.

EYE TWITTER

Eat celery or green leaf vegetables.

FAT—OVERWEIGHT

SYMPTOMS: Too heavy

CAUSE: Eating too much for the amount of physical labor performed and eating too late at night.

TREATMENT: Eat a good strong breakfast like a dinner at 6 AM. Eat or drink nothing between meals except water. Eat a good lunch at 12 noon. Eat or drink nothing but water until breakfast the next morning. This program will cause you to gain strength and loose weight.

FAT (CORPULENT)

"Closely apply their minds to books and eat the allowance of a laboring man. Under such habits some grow corpulent, because the system is clogged. Others become lean, feeble and weak because their vital powers are exhausted in throwing off the excess of food." 3T 490.

You are digging your grave with your knife fork and spoon.

FEET—COLD

The arms and legs should be kept as warm as the forehead.

F

If they are not they just do not have enough covering on them. Don't sit with cold feet put on more leg covering and warm boots or shoes, then get some vigorous exercise.

FEET AND LEGS SWELLING

SEE: Dropsy

FEVER—STOP EATING

"In case of severe fever, abstinence from food for a short time will lessen the fever, and make the use of water more effectual. While the fever is raging, food may irritate and excite the blood but as soon as the strength of the fever is broken, nourishment should be given in a careful, judicious manner." HL 921.

—NATURE'S EFFORT

"Nature, to relieve herself of poisonous impurities, makes an effort to free the system, which effort produces fevers and what is termed disease." HL 906.

"Nature bears abuse as long as she can without resisting, then she arouses, and makes a mighty effort to rid herself of the encumbrances and evil treatment she has suffered. Then come headache, chills, fevers, nervousness, paralysis, and other evils." HL 907.

—WATER

"Reduce the feverish state of the system by a careful and intelligent application of water." HL 918.

F

FLU (INFLUENZA) OR (GRIPPE)

SYMPTOMS: Comes suddenly, victim feels sick and unwilling to work or play. Much like a common cold except less nose running and greater weakness. Headache, drowsiness, ache all over, chills and low fever.

CAUSE: Lowered resistance. Disobeying the 8 laws of health.

TREATMENT: Give sea water bowel cleansing or 3 high enemas. Give sweat bath. Drink lots of warm water.

HERBS: Spoonful of red cayenne pepper in water, cold. Stop burning with oil. Cooking oil.

FOOD—TRAVELING

"When traveling, some are almost constantly nibbling, if there is anything within their reach. This is a most pernicious practice." HL 394.

FOOD POISONING

Take warm water, add one tablespoonful of salt to the quart. Drink till you vomit or it goes on through the bowels. Follow with fresh water. Take charcoal powdered, in water, or in a little olive oil every 1/2 till pain is relieved

FOOT—NAIL IN FOOT

1. Pull out the nail.
2. Encourage bleeding to help cleanse the wound.
3. Put turpentine or balsam or thin pine pitch deep in the hole.

G

4. For red swelling or blood poisoning with red streaks, put in hot water for about 5 minutes then into ice cold water for about one minute. Keep this up till skin becomes mottled, red and white. Repeat as necessary.

FOOT TROUBLE—PLANTAR WARTS ON BOTTOM OF FEET

SYMPTOMS: Very painful warts on the bottom of the feet. Grow rapidly.

CAUSE: UNKNOWN

TREATMENT: Crush wood sorrel or sheep sorrel and apply a poultice for several days, changing poultice morning and night. As color changes apply a little cooking oil and gently lift out wart.

Also a slice of lemon on the wart for several days is an old remedy.

G

GALL STONES

SYMPTOMS: Skin turns yellow at times. Sudden excruciating agony as stone attempts to pass out through the gall-duct. Pain stops suddenly. Lasts for a few minutes to a few days. The pain is on the upper part of the abdomen on the right side. Danger to life small.

CAUSE: Eating grease and fatty foods, butter, rich foods, fat meats, too much starch, sugar, milk, eggs, cheese, soda, drinks, lack of water.

TREATMENT: Stop breaking the laws of health. Eat raw foods. Give tablespoonful olive oil and a teaspoonful of lemon juice every 1/2 hour till relieved.

Grapefruit or orange rind (unsprayed), boil 20 minutes. Take 3 glassfuls daily.

Apply heat to sore place will often dislodge stone and give speedy relief.

HERBS: Smart weed tea (water pepper), 3 cups daily will dissolve stones.

GANGRENE

Mortification, putrefaction of soft tissue.

CAUSE: Severe inflammation on open sore with offensive odor. The body is full of toxins with a sick blood stream.

TREATMENT: Cleanse the bowels, cleanse the blood stream. Drink pure water, breathe fresh air. Eat 80% raw foods. Drink 3 cups of soy bean coffee daily. (Roast soy beans. Then drink) when diabetes. (See diabetes).

GAS (ON STOMACH OR LOWER BOWELS)

SYMPTOMS: Belching or passing gas, swelling

CAUSE: Wrong combinations of food. Eating in between meals. Eating when under mental or physical strain, too tired.

TREATMENT: Clean out the bowels, take charcoal. Drink charcoal water. Poultice of charcoal over belly.

GOITER—ENLARGEMENT OF THYROID GLAND IN NECK

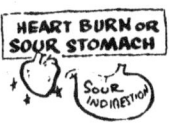

SYMPTOMS: Bulging eye-balls, bleed easily, fingers tremor, hands shake,

G

vomiting and diarrhea, heavy sweating, nervous irritability, skin eruptions, get very thin.

CAUSE: Lack of sea weeds and sea water. A starvation of the 97 elements in the diet.

TREATMENT: Cleanse the bowels, cleanse the blood stream. Keep a full 6 hours between meals. Eat sea weeds as kelp, dulse etc. Take sea water in lemon juice with each meal.

GONENESS

"The stomach becomes weary by being kept constantly at work disposing of food not the most healthful. Having no time for rest, the digestive organs become enfeebled, hence the sense of 'goneness' and desire for frequent eating." HL 679.

GOUT

SYMPTOMS: A very sore sensitive big toe and joints

CAUSE: Excessive uric acid in the blood and deposits in around the joints.

TREATMENTS: Stop alcohol, tobacco, meat, coffee, highly spiced foods, sugar and vinegar. Eat natural simple food. Stop suppers.

GLAUCOMA

Disease of eye by increase of pressure.

Obey God's 8 laws of health carefully.

Go barefoot and work toes into small gravel.

H

HAPPY

"Those who are always busy, and go cheerfully about the performance of their daily tasks, are the most happy and healthy." CH 53.

HAY FEVER

SYMPTOMS: A catarrhal inflammation of the nose and eyes. Watery discharges from the eyes, cold in the head, headache, tickling in the nose, sneezing, coughing, distressed breathing.

CAUSES: Bad habits of eating is the biggest cause; the body is loaded with toxins and the bowels and blood are dirty.

TREATMENT: Cleanse the bowels with sea water. Obey carefully the 8 laws of health.

HAIR—ARTIFICIAL

"The artificial hair and pads covering the base of the brain heat and excite the spinal nerves centering in the brain. The head should ever be kept cool. The heat caused by these artificial coverings induces the blood to the brain. The action of the blood upon the lower or animal organs of the brain, causes unnatural activity, tends to recklessness in morals, and the mind and heart are in danger of being corrupted." HL 775.

HEADACHE

CAUSE: Many; constipation, eye strain, bump, nervous tension, wrong eating habits, hangover, coffee and tea, drugs, sprays, preservatives, etc.

H

GET THEM INTO THE SHADE QUICK.

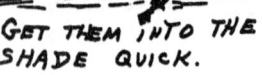

KEEP ARMS AND LEGS WARM

TREATMENT: Stop breaking the 8 laws of health. Clean out the bowels. Relax from stress and strain.

HEALTH

"A person whose mind is quiet and satisfied in God is in the pathway to health." HL 1012.

"He who is at peace with God has secured the most important requisite to health." HL 1003.

HEAT EXHAUSTION (SUN STROKE)

SYMPTOMS: Face flushed, skin dry and hot, pulse rapid and full, temperature high, headache some times unconsciousness.

CAUSE: Lack of the 97 elements found in sea water and sea weeds in the blood stream.

TREATMENT: Give sea water to drink and cayenne pepper while conscious. Water to drink. Rub arms and legs toward heart. Pray.

HEART PALPITATION

"Naked extremities.... The circulation is not equalized.... Producing palpitation of the heart, on account of too much blood in that locality." HL 773.

"The liver, heart, and brain are frequently affected by drugs." HL 866.

Sugar, tobacco, alcohol, overeating, tea and coffee cause diseases of the heart.

H

HEART TROUBLE

SYMPTOMS: Breath shortness after slight exertion, pain or tightness in chest, often running down left arm. Ankles or abdomen swelling. Breathing bent forward, needing several extra pillows to sleep on.

CAUSE: Breaking the laws of health. Fat, grease, butter, meat, over-eating, blood, etc.

TREATMENT: Take 1/2 glass of cold water with 1/4 teaspoon of cayenne pepper (no black pepper it is poison to the heart) repeat as needed. This will generally stop a heart attack in a few seconds. Apply ice to the heart and heat to the hands and feet. Cleanse the bowels. Don't over-eat or eat in between meals.

HEMORRHAGE

SYMPTOMS: Bleeding internally or externally. Spitting blood, bloody stools.

TREATMENT: Give cayenne pepper (red) in a little water.

HEMORRHOIDS—PILES

SYMPTOMS: Swollen veins, just inside or outside the anus. Difficult bowel movements, itching, bleeding, pain.

CAUSE: Constipation, hard overdue bowel movements. Straining at stools. Wrong diet of refined food.

TREATMENT: Correct constipation. Eat more roughage and small seeds. Apply ice for one hour if you can stand it. Insert olive oiled clove of garlic into the rectum at night. Expel in the morning. Kerosene is a good remedy.

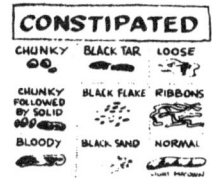

HERPES

SEE: Shingles

HICCUP (HICCOUGH)

TREATMENT: Plug ears with fingers. Hold nose closed. Drink rapidly 2 or 3 glasses of cold water (you will need help). This is very successful.

HIVES

SYMPTOMS: Itching in swelled spots all over skin.

CAUSE: Body too acid.

TREATMENT: Eat a lot of green leaf foods.

HIGH BLOOD PRESSURE

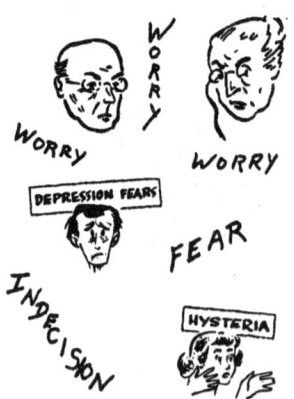

SYMPTOMS: Blood pressure above normal range. Roughly 100 plus your age is average. Lower for vegetarians, non smokers, non alcoholics or coffee and tea drinkers. Often brings on stroke.

CAUSE: Anything that constricts the flow of blood causes the pressure to go up. Heavy blood filled with toxins and a loaded liver. Constipation.

TREATMENT: Cleanse the bowels. Eat 80% raw food. Relax your mind. Stop worrying. Trust God. Eat garlic one day a week with parsley.

H

HOOKWORM

SYMPTOMS: An internal bloodsucker found in hot climates. Worms 1/4 to 1/2 inch long. Lives in the small intestines. They feed on the blood sucked from the intestinal walls.

Anemia, lack of ambition, weakness, pale, hungry all the time. The female can lay up to 15,000 eggs a day. These pass out and in a warm climate hatch on the ground. The larvae will go through intact skin. Barefoot favors the entrance in mud between the toes. Shoes are good protection. Also food and water may infect.

TREATMENT: Cleanliness. 4 days orange juice only every 4 hours. Papaya skin juice is good in the orange juice. Charcoal or charcoal in olive oil. Hookworm will leave in 2 to 7 years. Keep clean.

HYDROPHOBIA (RABIES)

CAUSE: A mad dog or animal bite.

SYMPTOMS: Incubation period 1 to 6 months. General illness, depressed mind, swelling near the bite. Swallowing and breathing muscles tighten up and spasm. Thirsty but can't drink. Panic at sight of water, death in 2 to 5 days.

TREATMENT: Quick make wound bleed freely. Wash wound and apply vinegar, turpentine or ammonia. Or burn the bite with a red hot iron. Hot steam bath as hot as possible or hot tub bath with ice to head and heart for several hours is very successful. Drink sea water. Put 1/2 a lemon over the wound.

I

No MATTER HOW YOU FEEL GO MAKE SOMEONE ELSE HAPPY. CHEER UP SOMEONE. BE KIND TO ANIMALS. SMILE AT EVERYONE. LOVE CHILDREN.

IMAGINATION

"I have met many who were really sufferers through their imagination. They lacked will power to rise above and combat disease of body and mind, and therefore they were held in suffering bondage." HL 990.

"The first work of those who would reform is to purify the imagination." SA 29.

Some people have very little will power but plenty of won't power.

"The imagination often misleads and when indulged, brings severe forms of disease upon the afflicted. Many die of diseases which are mostly imaginary." CH 95.

"Thousands are sick and dying around us who might get well and live if they would but their imagination holds them. They fear that they will be made worse if they labor or exercise, when this is just the change they need to make them well." HL 989.

INSOMNIA (CAN'T SLEEP)

CAUSE: A disturbed mind. Unequal circulation. Pain. Sick.

TREATMENT: Clear your mind by reading your Bible. Or hold your mind on one thing in bed like a nail or a brick or a broom and don't let your mind wonder away from it. The mind will soon get tired and you will fall asleep.

Equalize the circulation with a hot or cold bath. Warm up cold hands and feet. Cool off if too hot.

HERBS: Cayenne pepper, catnip, hops in an herb tea induces sleep.

INSANITY

"Thousands are today in insane asylums whose minds became unbalanced by novel reading." HL 842.

"Sickness of the mind prevails everywhere. Nine tenths of the diseases from which men suffer have their foundation here. The religion of Christ, so far from being the cause of insanity, is one of its most effectual remedies; for it is a potent soother of the nerves." HL 1008.

Not all constipated people are insane but nearly all insane people have one form or another of bowel blocking.

TREATMENT: Cleanse the bowels. Obey the laws of health. MANY ARE RESTORED.

INSECT STINGS—BITES

1. Spider, centipede, scorpion, bee or others. Remove stinger if still in.

2. Apply charcoal and mud poultice.

3. Black widow spider bite. Suck it out, then apply charcoal and mud poultice. Hot baths or steam baths for abdominal pains after spider bite.

Snake bite and sting of reptiles and poisonous insects could often be rendered harmless by the use of charcoal poultice. P of H 26.

INVALIDS

"Outdoor life is the only medicine that many invalids need." CH 170.

For invalids who have feeble lungs, nothing can be worse than an overheated atmosphere.

Invalids who can should engage in light, useful labor in the open air a portion of each day doing a little more work each day. Walk a little farther each day.

"Self-made invalids dying by inches, dying by indolence, a disease which n one but themselves can cure." HL 594.

J

JAUNDICE

SYMPTOMS: Skin and eyes turn yellow, urine is dark, Bowel movements light, bitter taste in mouth, constipation.

CAUSES: Overloaded liver, dirty blood stream from too much fat or oily foods.

TREATMENT: Stop all meat, milk eggs, butter, grease, nuts, sugar. Cleanse the bowels with sea water. Go on diet of raw fruits, grains and vegetables. Keep a full 6 hours in between meals.

JOINTS

"The disease which the drug was given to cure may disappear, but only to reappear in a new form such as painful, diseased joints." HL 778.

K

KIDNEY AND BLADDER

INFECTION: Corn silk tea. Ripe lemon water (nothing else) without sugar or honey for 5 days.

KIDNEY STONES: Smart weed tea dissolves stones. Juniper berries; 4 berries first day. 5 berries second day. 6 berries 3rd day. Up to 12th day. Continue 15 berries for 5 days, then one less each day. Chew the berries.

KIDNEY TROUBLE: Cleanse with sea water the bowels. Drink lots of corn silk tea.

LOW BLOOD PRESSURE

Undernourished, tired, lack of good red blood, not enough fresh air, sunshine, good food.

L

LEUKORRHEA (THE WHITES)

CAUSE: Mostly cold arms and legs

TREATMENT: Put on warm clothes on the arms and legs. Keep the wrists and ankles as warm as the forehead.

Half the diseases of women are caused by unhealthful dress. There is but one woman in a 1000 who clothes her limbs as she should. Women should clothe her limbs as thoroughly as do men. HL 548.

L

UNCLEAN MEATS

NO TOBACCO

NO COFFEE

RAW FOODS ONLY FOR 1 YEAR. AN ANGEL GAVE THIS INSTRUCTION AND SHE RECOVERED.

LEPROSY—PORK

The eating of pork has produced scrofula, leprosy and cancerous humors. Pork-eating is still causing the most intense suffering to the human race. In a warm climate eating pork often produces leprosy. In a cool climate pork eating produces cancers.

LEPROSY (HANSENS' DISEASE)

There are two kinds of leprosy. One causes large nodules under the skin and often become ulcers. Spreading, disease runs 5-10 years. Second kind of leprosy affects the nerves causing large white patches, dead in feeling. Parts shrivel up and fall off. Disease runs 20-30 years.

Only flesh eaters can get leprosy. Vegetarians are never known to get the disease even with close contact. Pork and crocodile eaters are very likely victims of leprosy in a hot climate. Read carefully in your Bible Lev. 7; and Lev. 11: and Moses will tell you how to keep from getting leprosy and cancer.

TREATMENT: Stop eating all pork, meat of all kinds, blood, fat, grease, butter, lard, sugar, tea, coffee, tobacco, alcohol. Obey the 8 laws of health and go on a diet of raw ripe fruit and vegetables, grains and nuts. 6 vegetables, 2 fruits, one sweet, one fat, food proportion of 10 daily.

USE CHAPARRAL TEA. LOTS OF IT.

LEUKEMIA—BLOOD CANCER

Sassafras tea.

CAUSE: DRUGS HAVE DESTROYED THE BLOOD making organs of the body. Mostly terminal.

TREATMENT: Stop drugs, obey all 8 laws of health. Give sun baths often it increases the blood 25%. Eat lots of green leafy vegetables and ripe fruits. It will take divine power to heal this disease.

LIVER

"Useful employment would bring into exercise the enfeebled muscles, enliven the stagnant blood in the system, and arouse the torpid liver to perform its work. The circulation of the blood would be equalized, and the entire system invigorated to overcome bad conditions." HL 593.

"All that is taken into the stomach above what the system can use to convert into good blood, clogs the machinery, for it can not be made into either flesh or blood and its presence burdens the liver." CH 160.

LIVER TROUBLE

Stop eating or drinking anything in between meals except water.

Keep a full 6 hours in between your meals.

Eat a lot of green leafy vegetables, eat sea weed daily.

Obey the 8 laws of health.

L

Go make someone else happy. Visit the sick. Cheer up the discouraged and you will not be lonely.

LONELINESS

"No relief until they shall come to Christ, the wellspring of life. Complaints of weariness, loneliness, and dissatisfaction will then cease. Satisfying joys will give vigor to the mind, and health and vital energy to the body." CH 241.

LOW BLOOD PRESSURE

CAUSE: Not enough good food, insufficient rest, lack of outdoor exercise, not enough red blood.

TREATMENT: Obey the 8 laws of health. Sun baths daily, increasing the time slowly, fresh air. Raw eggs beat up in unsweetened grape juice, taken twice daily.

Use a little cayenne pepper with your food for a while.

LUNGS—OPEN WINDOWS

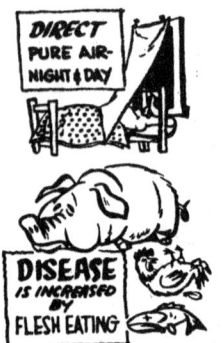

Those who have excluded the air from their sleeping rooms should commence to change their course immediately. They should let in air by degrees and increase its circulation until they can bear it winter and summer with no danger of taking cold. The lungs in order to be healthy, must have pure air.

LUNG TROUBLE—MEAT EATING

Cancers, tumors, and pulmonary diseases are largely caused by meat eating. CH 133.

Morning exercise in walking, or cultivating, is the surest, safeguard against congestions of the brain and lungs. HL 574.

"For invalids who have feeble lungs, nothing can be worse than an over-heated atmosphere." HL 715.

Stove heat destroys the vitality of the air, and weakens the lungs. P.of H. 21.

Open fire place is best.

M

MALARIAL FEVER

"Take pulverized charcoal, put water upon it, and give this water to the sick man to drink, putting bandages of charcoal over the bowels and stomach." P of H 23.

"Pulverized charcoal is one of the very best and most effectual remedies for the stomach—anything like malaria—to eat dry or in hot water." Letter 119 E.G.W. 1896.

MALARIA

SYMPTOMS: Chills and shaking followed by fever and high temperature.

CAUSE: The bite of one kind of mosquito that has sucked blood from a malaria infected person.

TREATMENT: Have steam bath ready and hot when the attack is expected. While in the chill give a steam bath before the fever starts. If done properly there is no more malaria unless you get a mosquito bite again. If you are too late with the heat, get it at the next chill.

M

OF MARRIED PEOPLE USE MODERATION

MARRIAGE

"It is frequently the case that old men choose to marry young wives. But thus doing the life of the wife has had to feel the want of that vitality which she has imparted to her aged husband. It is still worse for young men to marry women considerable older than themselves. The offspring of such unions is in many cases, where age widely differ, have not well balanced minds." SA 67.

"Those who are seriously deficient in business tact, and who are the least qualified to get along in the world, generally fill their houses with children. Those who are not qualified to take care of themselves, should not have children." SA 63.

—BASE PASSION

"No man can truly love his wife if she will patiently submit to become his slave and minister to his degraded passions." SA 44.

—TOO YOUNG

"Attachments formed in childhood have often resulted in a very wretched union, or in a disgraceful separation." SA 11.

—COUNSELOR

"If there is any subject which should be carefully considered and in which the counsel of older and more experienced persons should be sought, it is the subject of marriage.

M

If ever the Bible was needed as a counselor, if ever divine guidance should be sought in prayer, it is before taking a step that binds persons together for life." PP 117.

—EXCESS

"The brain nerve—power is squandered by men and women because called into unnatural action to gratify base passions." SA 44.

—SEX

"Many have no strength at all to waste in this direction. They have already, from their youth up, weakened their brains and sapped their constitutions by the gratification of their animal passions." SA 49.

"Lock the faults of one another within your own hearts." SA 58.

—SEX, MARITAL EXCESS

"God requires them to control their married lives from any excesses. But very few feel it to be a religious duty to govern their passions. They reason that marriage sanctifies the indulgence of the baser passions. God holds them accountable for the expenditure of vital energy, which weakens their hold on life and enervates the entire system." SA 43.

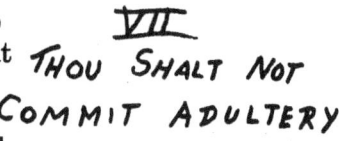

—MEMORY—ILL—CHOSEN READING

"The memory is greatly injured by ill-chosen reading, which has a tendency to unbalance the reasoning powers, and to create nervousness, weariness of the brain, and prostration of the entire system." HL 843.

M

MEAT EATING

"The liability to take disease is increased tenfold by meat eating." HL 454.

"Something must be prepared to take the place of meat, and these foods must be well prepared, so that meat will not be desired." HL 440.

"There are but few animals that are free from disease." HL 474.

—FISH

LEVITICUS 7 AND 11 THE ENTIRE CHAPTERS TELL YOU WHAT GOD SAYS ABOUT IT.

"In many localities even fish is unwholesome, and ought not be used. This is especially so where the fish come in contact with the sewage of large cities. The fish that partake of the filthy sewage of the drains may pass into waters far distant from the sewage, and be caught in localities where the water is pure and fresh, but because of the unwholesome drainage in which they have been feeding, they are not safe to eat." HL 480.

—BLOOD

"For whosoever eateth the fat of the beast, even the soul that eateth it shall be cut off from His people."—(Heart failure)

"Moreover ye shall eat no manner of blood, whatsoever should it be that eateth any manner of blood even that soul shall be cut off from His people." (heart failure) Leviticus 7:25, 26, 27.

"Dispense with animal food, and use grains, vegetables and fruits as articles of diet." SA 22.

M

"Among those who are waiting for the coming of the Lord, meat eating will eventually be done away; flesh will cease to form a part of their diet." CT & BH 119.

—PORK

"The eating of pork has produced scrofula, leprosy, and cancerous humors. Pork-eating is still causing the most intense suffering to the human race." Disease and Its Causes 14.

MEASLES

Incubation 7 to 14 days.

SYMPTOMS: It comes on like a bad cold and gets worse. Runny nose, eyes water and red. Cough dry. fever a little more each day to 3rd or 4th day. White spots 3rd day inside mouth. Red rash 4th day normally begins back of ears. Red spots scab over. (Don't scratch off scabs or it may leave pock marks). Improvement usually rapid. Keep in bed 2 days after fever goes down. Measles catches easily if your body is low. Usually only once.

TREATMENT: Cleanse bowels, sweat baths, drink lots of water. Breathe fresh air.

MENSTRUATION

Monthly period, menses. The periodic discharge of blood from the vagina. Normally girls begin in early teens and continue except during pregnancy or disease until late forties or early fifties.

M

MENOPAUSE—CHANGE OF LIFE

Comes on anywhere in life from early forties to late fifties. It is a normal event in life and need not be feared. Eighty five women out of a hundred have no trouble at all. Some have a few hot flashes that last a minute or two. The best years of life are often experienced after menopause.

TREATMENT: A happy frame of mind and good health habits. Keep arms and legs warm. 3 bowel movements daily. Eat good food.

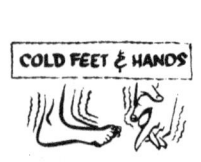

MENSES TROUBLES

Put on more clothes on arms and legs. Keep feet warm. Keep wrists and ankles as warm as the forehead.

MIND—INSANE

"Thousands are today in insane asylums whose minds became unbalanced by novel reading." HL 842.

"The consciousness of right-doing is the best medicine for diseased bodies and minds." HL 1003.

"In nine cases out of ten the knowledge of a sin-pardoning Saviour would make them better both in mind and body." HL 1009.

In the use of rake and hoe and spade they will find relief for many of their maladies. Idleness is the cause of many diseases.

M

MOUTH—BAD TASTE

"If more food is eaten than can be digested and appropriated, a decaying mass accumulates in the stomach, causing an offensive breath, and a bad taste in the mouth." HL 399.

MIND

"Nothing is so fruitful a cause of disease as depression, gloominess and sadness." HL 66.

"In order to preserve the balance of the mind, labor and study should be united." CH 179.

"If you are in constant fear that your food will hurt you, it most assuredly will." HL 999.

MOUTH SORE: CANKER

Sore spots in mouth and on tongue.

CAUSE: Eating too many fruits, grains, starches.

TREATMENT: Eat lots of green leafy foods. Red raspberry leaf tea will also heal up sore spots quickly.

Diet should be 6 vegetables, 2 fruits, 1 fat food and 1 sweet food to keep in balance.

FOOD BALANCE

6 VEGETABLES
2 FRUITS
1 FAT FOOD
1 SWEET FOOD
———
10

MULTIPLE SCLEROSIS (M.S.)

"MANY SCARS"

A crippling disease of the nervous system.

The covering around the nerve wires degenerates in patches and is filling in with car tissue. Not contagious.

M

SYMPTOMS: The nerves are "short circuited" causing the staggering walk, vision double or blurred, shaking, pins feeling, speech slurred, bowel and bladder troubles.

CAUSE: Breaking God's 8 laws of health. Obey all of them and the nerves will slowly heal.

TREATMENT: Cleanse the bowels. Take steam baths. Eat 80% raw food. Eat sea weeds daily. Sunflower seeds, coconuts, avocados, raw peanuts.

MUMPS—CONTAGIOUS

Most often a childhood disease, but when adults get it they can get very sick. Men and older boys can get it down in the testicles causing them to dry up and become sterile. (Rub with turpentine and keep exposed to the air so it won't blister.) Heals quickly. In women the ovaries can get involved.

SYMPTOMS: Swelling of the glands under ear and down under jaw, spreading to the other side in a few days. Disease runs a course of 7 to 10 days.

CAUSE: Disease is an effort of nature to free the system from a violation of the laws of health. Cleanse bowel, skin, eat raw food. STAY IN BED 5 days after swelling goes down or it may go into the testicles.

NERVES

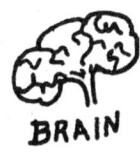
BRAIN

"Tea has an influence to excite the nerves, and coffee benumbs the brain; Both are highly injurious. HL 487.

"You should use the most simple food, prepared in the most simple manner, that the fine nerves of the brain be not weakened, benumbed, or paralyzed." 2T 46.

"For nervous, gloomy, feeble patients, outdoor work is invaluable. They will find relief for many of their maladies." CH 166.

"The bath is a soother of the nerves." CH 104.

A cup of catnip herb will quiet the nerves. Tobacco poisons the nerves.

NERVE TREATMENT

Cleanse the bowels, take steam baths, drink water, eat properly, go to bed at dark, relax at your work, (you get more work done), live in the open air, take your sleeping bag and sleep on the ground (dig a little hole for your hips.) Massage out the lumps and tight cords in the back of the neck.

NERVE RELAXING HERBS: Catnip, hops, cayenne pepper, lobelia tea.

NEPHRITIS (INFLAMMATION OF KIDNEYS)

Corn silk tea, shave grass tea, slippery elm bark. In bad cases use nothing but ripe lemon water for 3-10 days.

N

Sugar is one of the biggest causes. Stop all sugars, refined salt, all refined foods.

Eat the foods the way God and nature put them together. Don't take them apart.

NEURALGIA (RHEUMATISM)

SYMPTOMS: A severe pain along a nerve in the part affected. Often eruptions along nerve line. Pain by spurts.

CAUSE: Toxins or poisons in the system. Decayed teeth throwing poison into the blood stream, clogged bowels.

TREATMENT: Cleanse bowels. Drink water. Hot and cold applied to sore part. Go on a diet of raw food for one week.

NEURALGIA 15—30—45

"Vice after 15 years of age will pay penalty for transgression of her laws especially from ages 30 to 45 by numerous pains in the system, such as; Affections of liver, lungs, neuralgia, rheumatism, affections of spine diseased kidneys, cancerous humors, sudden breaking down and death." SA 20.

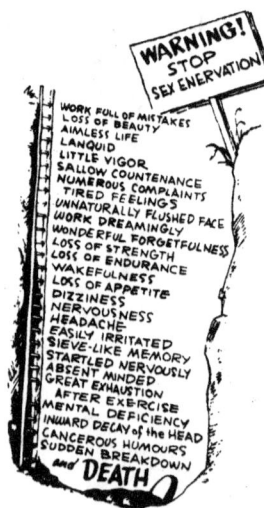

"Dampness gathers in the house, especially in wet seasons the sleeping rooms become damp, and those who sleep in the beds are troubled with rheumatism, neuralgia and lung complaints, which generally end in consumption." HL 615.

NIGHT RISING TO URINATE

Stop eating bread and mushes, cereals, stop using cow's milk. Drink parsley root tea 3 times daily.

NIGHT SWEATS

Strong sage tea. Give big spoonful 3 times a day, with double dose at bedtime. Or use cinquefoil (5 finger fern) root tea as above.

NOSE BLEED

"When the extremities, which are remote from the vital organs are not properly clad, the blood is driven to the head, causing headache or nosebleed." 2T 531.

"Children with extremities naked ... the circulation is not equalized.... The blood is driven to the head, causing headache or nose bleed." HL 773.

TREATMENT: Lay on your back for 5 minutes will nearly always stop it. Drink a little cayenne pepper in cold water will stop bleeding anywhere in the body. Stop mouth burning with a little cooking oil.

O

OPIUM

"The only safe course is to touch not, taste not, handle not ... Tea, coffee, wines, tobacco, opium and alcoholic drinks." HL 505.

OVER EATING

"Overeating is intemperance just as surely as is liquor drinking." HL 406.

"Over-eating has a worse effect upon the system than overworking." HL 405.

"The brain nerve energy is benumbed and almost paralyzed by over-eating." HL 689.

O

THEY COULD EAT THE SAME AMOUNT OF FOOD.

—STOMACH

"It becomes debilitated, the digestive organs are weakened, the disease with all its train of evils, is brought on as the result." HL 260.

"Some grow corpulent, because the system is clogged, others become thin and feeble because their vital powers are exhausted in throwing off the excess of food. The liver is burdened." CT & BH 160-1.

"No matter what the quality of the food, (over-eating) clogs the living machine, and thus hinders it in its work." CT & BH 51.

"Nearly all the members of the human family eat more than the system requires. This excess decays, and becomes a putrid mass.... If more food, even of a simple quality, is placed in the stomach than the living machinery requires, this surplus becomes a burden, the system makes desperate efforts to dispose of it, and this extra work causes a tired feeling. Some who are continually eating call this 'all gone' feeling hunger, but it is caused by the over worked condition of the abused digestive organs." HL 685.

OVER WORK

"When we overtax our strength, and become exhausted, we are liable to take cold, and at such times there is danger of disease assuming a dangerous form." HL 279.

"By neglecting to take physical exercise, by overworking mind or body, we unbalance the nervous system." CH 41.

P

OVERWEIGHT

SEE: Over-eating

"They (ministers, students, etc.) closely apply their minds to books, and eat the allowance of a laboring man. Under such habits, some grow corpulent (fat) because the system is clogged. Others become lean (thin) feeble and weak, because their vital powers are exhausted in throwing off the excess of food; The liver becomes burdened, and unable to throw off the impurities in the blood." HL 686.

CAUSE: Little or no breakfast, eating between meals, light lunch, coffee breaks, and a heavy meal at night with a few extra snacks before going to bed puts on an overload of unhealthy weight.

TREATMENT:
1. Eat a heavy breakfast at 6 in the morning and be finished before 7 a.m.
2. Eat or drink nothing in between meals except water.
3. Eat a good lunch or dinner at 12 noon and be all finished before 1 P.M.

4. Again eat or drink nothing in between meals except water.
5. <u>NO SUPPER</u>. Take a drink of water and go to bed and you will lose weight and gain strength.

P

PAINFUL, DISEASED JOINTS

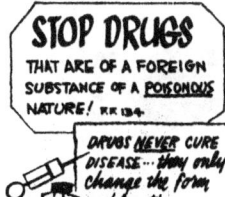

"The disease, which the drug was given to cure may disappear, but only to reappear in a new form, such as skin diseases, ulcers, painful, diseased joints and sometimes in a more dangerous and deadly form." HL 807.

PAIN—TO RELIEVE

"Pulverized charcoal in a bag used in fomentations.... If wet in smartweed, boiled, it is still better." P of H 24.

"Hop poultices over the stomach will relieve pain." P of H 6.

Poultice of mud and charcoal will relieve pain quickly. American Indian way of shorting out pain.

Put fingers of one hand on pulse of neck the other hand fingers on the pain. A few pulse beats will be generally felt as pain goes away. Will stop most pain for an hour or more.

PALE AND FEEBLE

"Close confinement indoors makes women pale and feeble, and results in premature death." HL 256.

PALPITATION OF HEART

"When the extremities are not properly clad the blood is driven to the head producing cough or palpitation of the heart, on account of too much blood in that locality." HL 552

"The second effect of tea drinking is headache, wakefulness, palpitation of the heart, indigestion, trembling of the nerves, with many other evils." CH 88.

PALSY—SHAKING

SEE: Also Parkinson's disease

SYMPTOMS: shaking of limbs, arms, hands, and head.

CAUSE: Drugs, tea, coffee, tobacco, flesh meats, white flour, polished rice, sugar, refined salt, refined foods of all kinds

TREATMENT: Stop using the refined foods. Eat raw fruit, grains, nuts and vegetables. Stop eating anything in between meals except water. Be sure to eat sea weeds every day to restore nerve force.

HERBS: Cayenne pepper, hops, catnip.

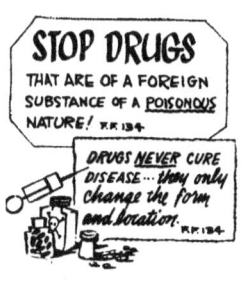

PARKINSON'S DISEASE (SHAKING PALSY)

SYMPTOMS: Fine tremor in hand or foot spreading till the entire body is involved. Face no expression. Slow measured speech. Falling forward or backward, numbness.

CAUSE: Chiefly a condition of the mind where everything must be in flawless perfect order or they are inwardly upset. They are all perfectionists that get the disease.

TREATMENT: The patient must realize the cause and relax with an "I DON'T CARE" attitude toward everything. The patient must keep saying "I DON'T CARE" about everything and laugh when things are out of place. Otherwise the mind disease is incurable. Follow the 8 laws of health. As fast as they change their perfectionist thinking they get well.

HERBS: Cayenne pepper, hop tea, catnip herb.

P

PARALYSIS:

SEE: Apoplexy

PASSIONS

"The less feverish the diet, the more easily can the passions be controlled. No eggs, meat, butter, vinegar, etc." HL 936.

PILES

SEE: Hemorrhoids

PIMPLES—SKIN ERUPTIONS—ACNE

CAUSE: Chief cause eating all kinds of good and bad food all day long.

REMEDY: Stop eating or drinking anything in between meals except water. Follow the laws of health.

PIN WORMS

White oak bark tea—expels.

Garlic in avocado

Worms have a tendency to leave a bowel where raw fruits and vegetables are largely eaten. Meat and cooked food encourages worms.

PLEURISY

SYMPTOMS: Sharp pains in the lung area at each large breath.

CAUSE: Sore inflamed lung cavity wall with insufficient lubrication causing the lung to stick to the rib cage and then tear loose with a sharp pain. An overload of poisons in the system.

P

TREATMENT: Follow the 8 laws of health. Hot and cold applied to chest and back, with 1 teaspoonful of cayenne pepper to every 3 pints of water fomentations.

POISON OAK OR IVY

If you get it try to avoid it. You can get it in many ways such as petting a dog that has been in it. Breathing the smoke of burning poison oak or ivy can be very dangerous.

Some say poison oak is a mind disease caused by fear.

SYMPTOMS: Red itching skin with blisters. Scratching spreads it. When you have been around it wash with soap right away.

TREATMENT: Lemon juice, drink and rub on. Juice of green edible leaves or hot coals or hot stove close as possible. BEST; Manzanita leaf tea inside and out often works wonders. What will do wonders for one person will not help another.

Stay away from it.

POISONING

A serious illness without fever. Induce vomiting if possible. Take 6 charcoal tablets every 1/2 hour. Swallow some raw eggs, milk, olive oil.

POISONOUS MEDICINES

Charcoal first. Tea of acorns and bark of white oak, resists the force of poisonous medicines.

WHITE OAK BARK

POISONOUS BITES

Charcoal and mud does wonders.

P

POISONOUS GAS INHALATION

Put 2 tablespoons of turpentine in a quart of boiling water and inhale vapor to counteract the effect of the poison gas.

POISON FOOD

Induce vomiting with warm salt water, or strong lobelia tea. Follow with 6 charcoal tablets and lots of water every 1/2 hour. Take 1/2 gal. of 1/3 sea water and 2/3 warm water.

POLIO (INFANTILE PARALYSIS)

A nerve disease which is a paralyzing and sometimes is crippling.

SYMPTOMS: Onset very much like a cold. Slight fever, not more than 3 days. Paralysis may or may not, develop at this time.

CAUSE: Cake, cookies, candy, ice cream, white bread, peeled potatoes, white sugar, devitalized salt. Taken apart foods. Cold arms and legs. Swimming too long in cold water. Till the lips get blue. Eating between meals.

TREATMENT: Obey 8 laws of health. Drink sea water and eat sea weeds. Eat natural food the way nature made them. Get at least 4 hours sleep before midnight.

PNEUMONIA

CAUSE: Pneumonia is an effort of nature to free the system from conditions that result from a violation of the laws of health.

P

Unhealthful conditions should be changed, wrong habits corrected. Then nature is to be assisted in her effort to expel impurities and to reestablish right conditions in the system.

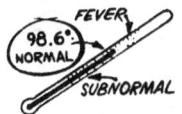

SYMPTOMS: Usually follows a neglected cold. Shaking, chills, high fever, sharp pains in the chest, sharper with deep breaths. Cough painful. Small blood spots in sputum.

TREATMENT: Cleanse the bowels. Give a steam bath. Give fresh AIR to breathe. Keep patient warm. Feel of hands and feet every 15 minutes and don't let them chill or they may die. Give warm water to drink. Apply hot fomentations and ice rub to chest and back. No stove heated air to breathe. They will live in a tent but die in a house. Don't get up too soon as a relapse is very dangerous.

HERBS: Blue vervain tea for sweating.

PREGNANCY

"The appetite of women in this condition may be variable, fitful and difficult to gratify. (Sea weeds or sea water will give the necessary 97 elements) the food should be nutritious, but should not be of an exciting quality." CH 77.

"Flesh-meats, pickles, spiced food or mince pies is a great mistake, and does much harm. The harm can not be estimated. If ever there is need of simplicity of diet and special care as to the quality of food eaten, it is in this important period." CH 78

P

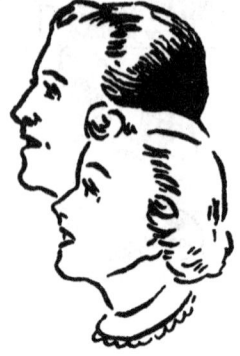

1st Month: Conception occurs. Count 280 days.

2nd Month: Nausea, vomiting, morning sickness, sleepiness, breasts sensitive, urination frequent.

3rd Month: Breasts get larger, very tired. A strange appetite that is satisfied by ocean water or sea weed.

4th Month: Gain in weight starts. Abdomen begins to show. Eat plenty of fruits and vegetables. At least 80% raw diet. Stay away from sugar, ice cream, candy, cake, cookies, soft drinks.

5th Month: The first movements will now be felt.

6th Month: Kicking may be strongly felt.

7th Month: Color of face may change, but it will be alright again after the birth.

8th Month: The enlarged veins will go away after birth.

Things will quiet down, just resting for birth. Take squaw vine tea, red raspberry leaf tea or mother wort tea.

9th month: The mother-to-be will feel fine as a rule but go to bed early. Get plenty of rest and don't overwork or get tired. Take lots of squaw vine tea; it helps make child birth wonderfully easy. Child settles 2 weeks before birth. Walking is very helpful, but don't get tired.

BIRTH: Should be under a lady doctor or mid-wife if possible or a good christian doctor. Baby should be given breast feeding right away not a bottle. It needs that first milk to be healthy.

P

PROSTATE TROUBLE

SYMPTOMS: Can't urinate freely or may stop the flow of urine entirely.

CAUSE: Gonorrhea, cancer, tuberculosis, a few men past 60 of age.

TREATMENT: To quickly start the flow of urine give hot and cold sitz baths. Stop all cooked food and eat raw, ripe fruit and vegetables with a small amount of nuts and sprouted seeds and grains. Follow the 8 laws of health.

HERBS: Corn silk tea in large quantities, or UVA URSI herb tea. Lots of parsley tea for one week.

PSORIASIS (CALLED A HEALTHY MAN'S DISEASE)

SYMPTOMS: Patches of reddish brown on the skin which soon cover with silvery-white scabs or dead skin which scale off. They range from very small to large places on scalp. Elbows, knees, legs and back. Sometimes come and go.

CAUSE: The skin is getting rid of toxins or poisons caused by a wrong diet and breaking God's 8 laws of health.

TREATMENT: Cleanse the bowels. Cleanse the blood stream. Obey strictly the 8 laws of health. Eat raw, ripe fruit and vegetables with sprouted grains and some nuts.

HERBS: Soft pine pitch or balsam applied to sores.

R

PTOMAINE POISONING
SEE: Food poisoning

PUFFINESS UNDER EYES
SEE: Kidney trouble. Use corn silk tea.

PULSE BEATS PER MINUTE

1 year	120
2 years	110
3 years	95
7 years	87
14 years	80-85
21 years	10-80
Normal adult	72

R

RABIES
SEE: Hydrophobia.

RATTLE SNAKE BITE
SEE: Snake bite.

REPININGS
"That which brings sickness of body and mind to nearly all is dissatisfied feelings and discontented repinings." HL 997.

RICKETS
Deformities of bone cause by a lack of elements and minerals.

SYMPTOMS: Enlarge liver and spleen causing a large belly. Badly formed teeth. Large head. Constipation.

TREATMENT: Cleanse the bowels and keep them moving 2 or 3 times daily. Give sweat baths and sun baths.

Stop all processed and taken apart foods as sugar, ice cream, candy, cookies, white rice, white flour products. Stop all eating or drinking anything between meals except water. Keep a full 5 or better 6 hours between meals. Go to sleep at 8 P.M.

HERBS: Sea weeds. Sea water daily.

RINGWORM (TINEA) A vegetable parasitic disease. No worm at all.

SYMPTOMS: Usually starts with a little pimple, which soon spreads and takes on its ringlike appearance, showing a circle of small scales. Hair in these patches becomes brittle and break off.

BANANA SKIN RUB ON IS VERY GOOD ALSO.

TREATMENT: Rub on tomato leaf juice. Black walnut skin juice rub on. Goldenseal, blood root. Kerosene—apply several times a day.

RHEUMATIC JOINTS

Wrap a swollen rheumatic joint in cloths wrung out of ice water, and the pain will almost instantly cease.

Follow the 8 laws of health. Cleanse the bowels. Check for bad teeth.

RHEUMATISM—DAMP HOUSE

"Dampness gathers in the house especially in wet seasons the sleeping rooms become damp, and those who sleep in the beds are troubled with rheumatism, neuralgia and lung complaints which generally end in consumption." HL 615.

S

RHEUMATISM

SEE: Arthritis

SYMPTOMS: Pain in the body muscles and sometimes joints.

CAUSE: Poisons in the system. Tea, coffee, tobacco, alcohol, candy, pie, ice cream, doughnuts, white bread, cakes, eating in between meals, sugar, starches, grease, lard, butter, pork, blood.

TREATMENT: Stop breaking God's 8 laws of health. Cleanse the bowels and bloodstream. Go on a diet of raw food for one week.

RHEUMATIC FEVER (NOT CONTAGIOUS)

SYMPTOMS: Twitching, jerky body movements, loss of weight or just don't grow. Fever low but persistent. Pale, bloodless skin. Often nose bleed from no apparent cause. Pains in the body, arms and legs. Great weakness.

CAUSE: White bread, white rice, sugar, candy, ice cream, tea, coffee, sugar water drinks. Eating and drinking anything in between meals except water. Constipation. Lack of fresh air, sunshine, exercise. Masturbation.

TREATMENT: Stop breaking the laws of health. Eat plenty of fruit, grains, nuts, and vegetables. Eat sea weeds daily.

S

SADNESS

"Nothing is so fruitful a cause of disease as depression, gloominess, and sadness." HL 66.

CURE: Make someone else happy.

S

SCALDS

SEE: Burns
Ice or cold water first, ocean water heals best.
Aloe Vera juice (the inside of leaf.)

Also grated raw potato poultice is good.

SCIENCE—BIBLE

"The Bible is not to be tested by mens ideas of science, but science is to be brought to the test of this unerring standard." HL 1185.

—TRUE

"Thus in simple language, we may teach the people how to preserve health, how to avoid sickness. This is true science." p of H. 13.

SCURVY (LACK OF RAW FOODS)

Eat sea weeds or drink sea water, lemons, oranges, potato peelings, raw cabbage, etc.

SEA SICKNESS (MOTION SICKNESS)

Eat lots of charcoal.

SEA SICKNESS

1. Take charcoal, it does wonders.
2. Place a piece of cardboard over the chest and stomach against the skin.

To stop motion sickness rub here as this is the reflex to the stomach.

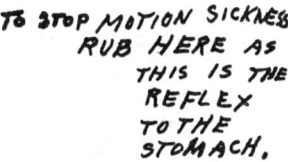

SHINGLES—HERPES, ZOSTER, TETTERS, ZONA

Same as a cold sore on the nerves
SYMPTOMS: A crop of small blisters along a nerve branch such as from the neck up over the face, or from the spine over the chest, or from lower spine around abdomen.

S

SEE: SPINE CORRECTION.

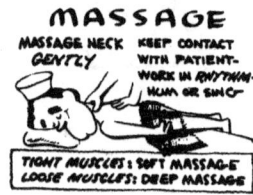

CAUSE: Spine nerve pinch (vertebra out of place), indigestion, nervous irritation, toxins or poisons in the system.

TREATMENT: Straighten the spine. Correct and follow the 8 laws of health.

SHOCK

SYMPTOMS: Face pale, sighing breaths, body cold, chill, vomiting.

CAUSE: Rapid fall in blood pressure. Injury, operations, electric shock. Emotional event or terrorizing event, overdose of drugs, loss of blood.

TREATMENT: Get patient warm, but not hot. Put the legs up above body. Massage arms and legs toward the heart gently, but firmly.

HERBS: Cayenne pepper 1/4 tsp. in a little water. (A little oil in the mouth will stop the burning). Ocean water, drink a little at a time.

SICKNESS

"Sickness is the result of violating natures' laws." CT, BH 12.

"It is a sin to be sick, for all sickness is the result of transgression." CH 37.

"In case of sickness, the cause should be ascertained, unhealthful conditions should be changed wrong habits corrected." MH 127.

"Sickness of the mind prevails everywhere. 9/10 (nine-tenths) of the diseases from which men suffer have their foundation here." HL 1008.

S

"God will not work a miracle to keep those from sickness who have no care for themselves, but are continually violating the laws of health, and make no effort to prevent disease." HL 1016

SICK ROOM

"The sick room, if possible, should have a draft of air through it, day and night. The draft should not come directly upon the invalid. While burning fevers are raging, there is but little danger of taking cold, but special care is needful when the crisis comes, and the fever is passing away." CH 56.

"Fresh air will prove more beneficial to the sick than medicine, and is far more essential to them than their food." HL 652.

"Every breath of vital air in the sick room is of the greatest value." HL 315.

"Those who cannot make themselves useful should be cautious in regard to visiting the sick." HL 660.

"All unnecessary noise and excitement should be avoided in the sick room." HL 659.

SILICOSIS

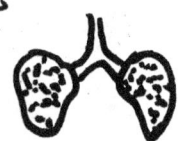

CAUSE: Inhalation of stone or sand dust, containing silicon dioxide.

TREATMENT: Nettle tea; drink lots of it. Also lobelia tea.

S

SKIN ERUPTIONS

"With many the poor, tired stomach may complain of weariness in vain. More food is forced upon it. The blood becomes impure, the complexion sallow, and eruptions frequently appear." HL 805.

SKIN—IMPURITIES

"Impurities are constantly and imperceptibly passing from the body, through the pores, and if the surface of the skin is not kept in a healthy condition, the system is burdened with impure matter." (Take sweat baths). HL 791.

SKIN DISEASES—DRUGS

"The disease, which the drug was given to cure may disappear, but only to reappear in a new form, such as skin diseases, ulcers, painful, diseased joints, and sometimes in a more dangerous and deadly form." HL 807.

SKUNK—STINK

Wash body and clothes with 1/2 cup of tomato juice in water, or ammonia 1/2 cup in water.

SLEEP—HOPS

"Hop tea will induce sleep. Hop poultices over the stomach will relieve pain." Place of Herbs page 4.

SMALLPOX—CONTAGIOUS 9-15 DAYS

A filth disease. Stopped by cleaning up the place and proper burying of human manure, sanitation, cleanliness.

S

SYMPTOMS: The skin reddens and many pimples like blisters form. Fever to 3rd day 103-104, goes away and comes again for 24 hours. Ten or 11 days starts getting better.

TREATMENT: Keep room darkened for light can damage the eyes. Cleanse the bowels. Cleanse the skin. Keep bed clothes clean. Give fresh air. Give water to drink lots of it. Steam baths. DO NOT SCRATCH as it will leave pock marks. For itching bathe skin in equal parts of lime water and olive oil. Yellow dock tea or golden seal tea stops pitting, use as a wash.

DON'T SCRATCH

SNAKE BITE

1. Quickly stop the blood from flowing back from the wound to the heart by a tight bandage, rope, shoestring, or something. Loosen slowly. Don't leave on too long.
2. Suck out the poison. Use a small glass or bottle drop a burning match in a bottle and place over the wound. The fire in the bottle burns up the air causing it to suck.
3. Wash freely with water.
4. A poultice of charcoal. "Snake bites and stings of reptiles and poisonous insects could often be rendered harmless by the use of charcoal poultices." P of H 26.
6. Put a bottle of turpentine on the bit until it turns green.
7. Mud or mud and charcoal is wonderful.
8. For a person bitten and swelling all over the body for some time: Remove all clothes and place in mud for 1-10 hours.
9. Pear cactus. Burns stickers off leaf, split and put on wound to ease pain.

WET CHARCOAL POULTICE

S

SODA

"Saleratus in any form should not be introduced into the stomach for the effect is fearful. It eats the coatings of the stomach, causes inflammation, and frequently poisons the entire system." HL 433.

SORE THROAT

CAUSE: Breaking the 8 laws of health. The lungs are throwing off a large amount of poisons which in passing make the throat sore.

TREATMENT: Obey the 8 laws of health. Cleanse the bowels. Breathe fresh air. Drink good water. Eat natural food.

SOUR STOMACH

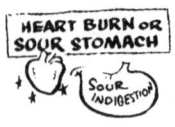

SYMPTOMS: A sour taste and burning coming from the stomach, sometimes called heartburn. Sour belching, indigestion, stomachache.

CAUSE: Eating between meals, not having a full six hours between meals, drinking anything but water between meals, coffee, tea, tobacco, flesh meats, sugar, candy, cakes, soft drinks, overeating, having too many kinds of food at one meal, mixing fruit and vegetables at one meal. Drinking water with meals.

TREATMENT: Obey the 8 laws of health. Keep 6 hours in between meals. Not one bite of food or drink between meals. Water only.

HERBS: Charcoal tablets. (Not activated).

S

SPIDER BITE

SEE: Snake bite. Suck out, apply mud and charcoal.

SPINE CORRECTION

Study carefully the following pictures and drawings. Start in very gently and practice on a friend. Then let him do it to you. GO EASY AND DON'T HURT ANYONE. Strong men need strong treatment BUT GO EASY ON SMALL MEN, women and children. Don't give thrusts! Push easy and massage gently like putting a kitten to sleep.

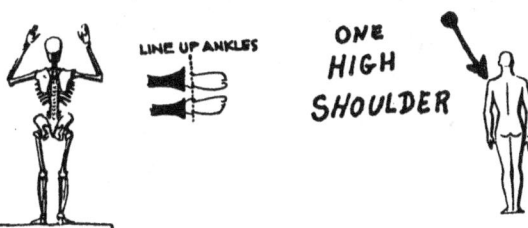

HIPS (SPINE CORRECTION)

1. Measure the ankles with the person lying perfectly straight, on their back.
2. If one leg is longer than the other find out if a bone has been broken and healed short or long.

SPINE CORRECTIONS

Study carefully the following pictures and drawings. Start in very gently and practice on a friend. Then let him do it to you. GO EASY AND DON'T HURT ANYONE. Strong men need strong treatment BUT GO EASY on small men, women and children. Don't give thrusts! Push easy and massage gently like putting a kitten to sleep.
Feel for tight muscles in neck and back.

S

Do this on each side. Do not push on shoulder, it hurts, push on chest close to shoulder.

Press on elbows, and rock back and forth so each bone in the back is touching the floor. Go easy.

This corrects the double slip. Do both sides.

As with all these treatments it is best to work in afternoon or evening, with a warm (not cold) person.

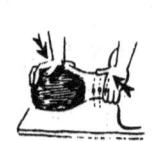

1, 2, 3, are 3 ways of doing nearly the same thing.

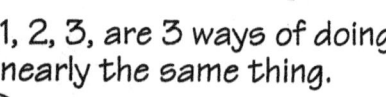

 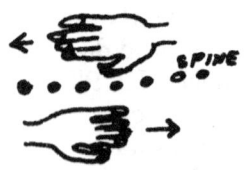 

Push gently and firmly, but no quick hard thrusts. Keep person at east. <u>DON'T HURT</u>.

S

Sometimes a hip gets out of socket a little. This will help put it back in place.

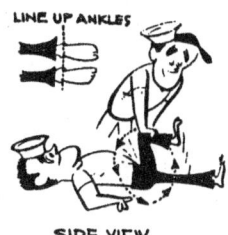
SIDE VIEW

TOP VIEW

Pull Straight

Two towels work fine, one under head, the other under chin, twisted over the

Stretching the spine. Start in very easy and slowly increase the pull at short pulls.

SPRAIN (VIOLENT TWIST OR PULL TO MUSCLES)

SYMPTOMS: Ligaments around joint torn or pulled. Red color turning dark.
TREATMENT: Cold water, ice or snow applied. Put on a tight bandage of elastic. Allow all the movement desired. Heat later stops pain and promotes healing. Mud and charcoal stops pain. Hot 3 minutes, cold 1/2 minute heals.
HERBS: Cayenne poultice.

STINGS—BEES, ETC.

SEE: Snake bite, Bee stings.

STONES

SEE: Gallstones, kidney stones.

STROKE

SEE: Apoplexy.

S

STOMACH, SOUR

SEE: Sour stomach

STOMACH—2 OR 3 KINDS OF FOOD

"It would be better to eat only two or three different kinds of food at one meal than to load the stomach with many varieties." HL 370.

—CHEESE

"Cheese should never be introduced into the stomach." (All kinds) HL 425.

—CHILDREN (PALE FACES)

In order to keep their restless children still, they have given them cake or sweets at almost any hour of the day, and their stomachs are crowded with hurtful things at irregular periods. Their pale faces testify to the fact that mothers are destroying their poor children.

—BAD BREATH

"If more food is eaten than can be digested and appropriated, a decaying mass accumulates in the stomach, causing an offensive breath, and a bad taste in the mouth." HL 399.

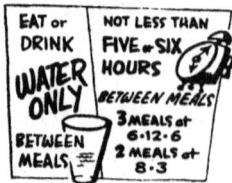

—EAT ALL DAY

"The stomach may be educated to desire food eight times a day, and feel faint if it is not supplied. But this is no argument in favor of so frequent eating." HL 388.

S

—TOO MUCH

"Nearly all the members of the human family eat more than the system requires." HL 400.

—CHILDREN

"Children are also fed too frequently, which produces feverishness and suffering in various ways. The stomach should not be kept constantly at work, but should have its periods of rest." HL 626.

—FERMENTATION

"So many varieties are introduced into the stomach that fermentation is the result, this condition brings on acute disease." HL 889.

"They eat when the system needs no food and at irregular intervals." CT & BH 50.

—LIQUID

"The more liquid there is taken into the stomach with the meals the more difficult it is for the food to digest." CT & BH 51.

—FOOD WASHED DOWN

Food should not be washed down. No drink is needed with meals. Eat slowly, and allow the saliva to mingle with the food.

—PAIN

"Take pulverized charcoal, put water upon it and give this water to the sick man to drink putting bandages of the charcoal over the bowels and stomach." P of H 23.

S

—HOT FOOD

"Very hot food ought not to be taken into the stomach. Soups, puddings, and other articles of the kind, are often eaten too hot, and as a consequence the stomach is debilitated. Let them become partly cooled before they are eaten." HL 414.

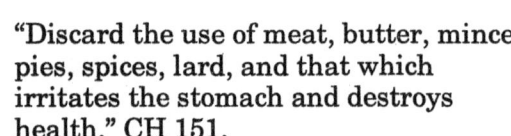

—PAIN

"Hop poultices over the stomach will relieve pain." Place of Herb page 4.

—IRRITANTS

"Discard the use of meat, butter, mince pies, spices, lard, and that which irritates the stomach and destroys health." CH 151.

—SLEEP

"When we lie down at night, the stomach should have its work all done, that it, as well as other portions of the body may enjoy rest." CT & BH 50.

—COLD WATER

"Taken with meals, water diminishes the flow of the salivary glands and the colder the water, the greater the injury to the stomach." HL 672.

—MASTICATION

"Thorough mastication is a benefit both to the teeth and the stomach." HL 664.

S

—WATER WITH MEALS

"Taken with meals, water diminishes the flow of the salivary glands and the colder the water the greater the injury to the stomach. Ice water or iced drinks with meals, will arrest digestion until the system has imparted sufficient warmth to the stomach to enable it to take up its work again." HL 409.

—MILK AND SUGAR

"Milk and sugar.... These clog the system, irritate the digestive organs and affect the brain." CH 150.

—FAST

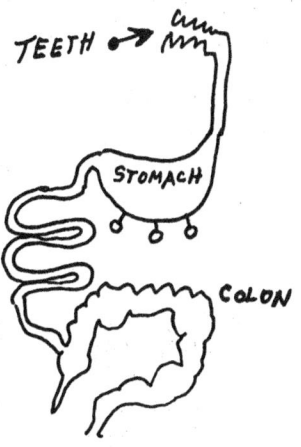

"That fast will prove to them of greater benefit than medicine, for the abused stomach will find that rest which it has long needed, and real hunger can be satisfied with plain diet." CH 148.

—RECOVERY

"The stomach may never recover health, but a proper course of diet will save further debility, and many will recover more or less, unless they have gone very far in gluttonous self murder." CH 148.

—WALK

"Exercise will aid the work of digestion. To walk out after a meal; Hold the head erect, put back the shoulders, and exercise moderately, will be a great benefit. The diseased stomach will find relief by exercise." HL 697.

S

FRUIT
GEN. 1:29

A FRUIT IS A SEED AND/OR A SEED POD. SOMETIMES YOU EAT THE SEED. SOMETIMES YOU EAT THE SEED POD. SOMETIMES YOU EAT BOTH THE SEED AND THE SEED POD.

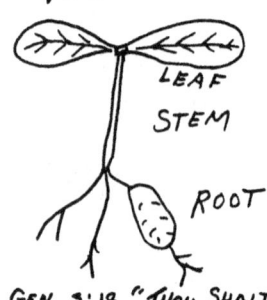

VEGETABLE
LEAF
STEM
ROOT

GEN. 3:18 "THOU SHALT EAT THE HERB OF THE FIELD".

IS THE FOOD A FRUIT OR A VEGETABLE

?

—FRUIT AND VEGETABLES

"If we would preserve the best health we should avoid eating vegetables and fruit at the same meal. If the stomach is feeble there will be distress. Have fruit at one meal and vegetables at the next.

—SODA

"Saleratus (soda) in any form should not be introduced into the stomach, for the effect is fearful. It eats the coating of the stomach causes inflammation, and frequently poisons the entire system." HL 433.

—TAXED

"Immediately after eating there is a strong draught upon the nervous energy. The brain force is called into active exercise to assist the stomach; therefore, when the mind or body is taxed heavily after eating the process of digestion is hindered." HL 667.

—GONENESS

"A feeling of goneness, a faintness, as though you must eat more. Nature is so thoroughly exhausted in consequence that you have this sensation of goneness, and you think that the stomach says: 'MORE FOOD,' when in its faintness, it is distinctly saying: 'GIVE ME REST.'" CH 157.

"Indigestion, dyspepsia. The work of digestion should not be carried on through any period of the sleeping hours." HL 668.

"The stomach must have its regular periods for labor and rest." HL 693.

"The remedy such required is to eat less frequently and less liberally, and be satisfied with plain, simple food, eating twice, or at most, three times a day." HL 695.

"Never let a morsel pass your lips between your regular meals." HL 392.

Keep a full 5 hours between meals, and 6 hours would be much better.

—TROUBLE

SOUR: Stop eating in between meals. Eat more green leaf vegetables.

GAS: Take charcoal. (Not activated)

ULCERS: Take cayenne pepper. Stop worrying. Eat young pine or fir shoots.

GNAWING PAIN: Stomach needs rest. Stop eating for a while.

BLEEDING ULCERS: Cayenne pepper.

CRAMPS: Mint tea. Charcoal.

STOMACH ACHE: Peppermint.

TONIC: Golden seal root.

GASTRIC, PEPTIC, DUODENAL ULCER: A sore in the stomach.

SYMPTOMS: Burning in the stomach, hunger pains—wanting to eat often to stop pain.

BLEEDING ULCERS: Vomiting blood or stools like black coffee grounds.

CAUSES: Worry, aluminum cooking utensils, nerve stress and strain, indecision, tobacco, alcohol, coffee, eating between meals.

BALANCING THE DIET

2 FRUITS
6 VEGETABLES
1 FAT FOOD
1 SWEET FOOD

MOST PEOPLE DON'T EAT ENOUGH VEGETABLES

S

TREATMENT: Slow down, relax, trust in God. Stop eating between meals. Take CAYENNE PEPPER to stop BLEEDING. Use cayenne with each meal (no black pepper). ULCERS: It is not so much what you eat that gives you ulcers as what is eating on you.

SUFFOCATION:

SEE: Drowning

SUGAR: The free use of sugar in any form tends to clog the system, and is not infrequently a cause of disease. CH 154.

SWELLING: LEGS, ANKLES

SEE: Edema

SUGAR
CAUSES:—
COLDS
FLU
PNEUMONIA
ARTHRITIS
RHEUMATISM
ROTS TEETH
DIABETES
ETC.

No WHITE SUGAR
No BROWN SUGAR
No RAW SUGAR
No MOLASSES

USE SWEET FRUITS
USE HONEY

A symptom, not a disease.

SWIMMING is good exercise. Everyone should learn how to swim. Swimming in cold water until the lips get blue does untold damage to the body, and lowers the resistance to polio and other diseases.

SYPHILIS

A venereal or "social" disease. Nearly always transmitted from one person to another by sexual intercourse.

SYMPTOMS: First a chancre (shanker) which looks like a small pimple up to an inch or so in size which may appear 9 days to 2 months after exposure. These will heal up as they spread syphilis all through the body in about 2 to 5 weeks. Next come rashes, skin diseases. Pain in the joints, tired, hair falls out a little in patches, fever.

The disease will sort of heal up, but is still alive in the system for 2 to 60 years. During this period it may appear like almost any disease. Tumors, brain diseases, nerve and spinal cord diseases, heart and blood diseases, skin trouble or bone decay, insanity, loss of memory. See a good doctor immediately. Follow the 8 laws of health.

SUN STROKE

SYMPTOMS: Face flushed, skin dry and hot, pulse rapid and full, temperature high, with unconsciousness, stop sweating.
CAUSE: Lack of the 97 elements in the blood stream, which also includes salt.
TREATMENT: Get person in the shade. Cool them down with cold water or ice. Give water to drink. Give sea water to drink which will build back the 97 elements. (later have them eat sea weeds) give small swallows of cayenne pepper in cold water, when they are awake, to prevent and take care of shock. Massage arms and legs toward the heart. Eat sea weeds and drink sea water in hot weather.

SUN STROKE

SEE: Heat Exhaustion

TAPE WORMS

Flat, thin, jointed worms found in the intestines. People get them by eating raw, or improperly cooked meat as, beef, pork, fish or eating or drinking food or water contaminated with dog, cat, cattle, sheep or human manure.

SEA WATER + CAYENNE PEPPER

DRINK A LITTLE SEA WATER EVERY DAY IN HOT WEATHER OR ON A HOT JOB.

WHEN WATER DOES NOT SATISFY THIRST YOU NEED A LITTLE SEA WATER.

T

SYMPTOMS: Sometimes a ravenous appetite with loss of weight. Anemia, diarrhea, nervous, weak, spasms, convulsions, fits, gritting the teeth when asleep.

TREATMENT: Malefern root, chew 5 times daily without food for 3 days. Or eat nothing but pumpkin seeds raw, for 3 days. Take sea water flush every morning.

TEA

"To a certain extent, tea produces intoxication. It enters into the circulation and gradually impairs the energy of body and mind. Tea draws upon the strength of the nerves, and leaves them greatly weakened, when its influence is gone.... Languor and debility corresponding to the artificial vivacity the tea imparted." CH 87. "Tea draws upon the strength of the nerves, and leaves them greatly weakened." HL 489.

TEETH

"Thorough mastication is a benefit both to the teeth and the stomach." HL 664.

TOOTH DECAY: Is caused by sugar, refined flour, refined salt, polished rice. Processed foods of all kinds. Any food from nature that man has taken apart. Eat the food the way God and nature made it grow.

TOOTHACHE: A little oil of cloves insert in the cavity. Powdered milk put in the hole will stop a toothache for a little while. Kerosene in the hole often affords immediate relief, pine pitch in a hole helps too.

T

SORE GUMS:
Brush teeth with golden seal and myrrh night and morning.

TESTICLES
SWOLLEN: Chickweed poultice. In mumps use application of turpentine, keep air all around or it will blister.

COLLECTING WATER:
SEE: Dropsy
Poultice of cabbage leaves.

TETTERS
SEE: Shingles

THIN (lean) FAT
Some grow corpulent, because the system is clogged. Others become lean, feeble and weak because their vital powers are exhausted in throwing off the excess of food. HL 686.
Over-eating is the hardest sin to break.

THROAT
SORE: Gargle with cayenne pepper in water.
Sore throat is caused by nature throwing out poisons (toxins) from the lungs. This makes the throat sore. Help nature expel toxins by cleansing the bowels, eat only raw food for a few days, take a sweat bath, drink lots of warm water.
CANCER OF THROAT: SEE: Cancer
WHITE THROAT: SEE: Diphtheria
RED AND WHITE THROAT:
SEE: Measles

THYROID TROUBLE
SEE: Goiter
Drink some sea water every day.
Eat sea weeds also daily.

T

STOP FILLING YOUR BODY WITH A BAD DIET. CLEAN OUT. FOLLOW THE LAWS OF HEALTH.

TONSILLITIS

SYMPTOMS: Sore, enlarged tonsils.

CAUSE: Breaking the 8 laws of health, eating between meals, candy, cake, cookies, ice cream, greasy food, meat, soft drinks, chewing gum, tea, coffee, etc.

TREATMENT: Stop breaking the 8 laws of health. Cleanse the body of sludge. Eat 2 meals a day, nothing between meals except water. Fruit at one meal and vegetables at the next, 80% raw.

They will clear up quickly on this treatment.

TUBERCULOSIS or T.B.

SEE: Consumption

TUMORS: A swelling or growth of tissue. They are not cancers, but a few of them become so. Tumors have many names, as fatty, fibrous, glandular, muscular, and cancerous. Tumors are garbage cans in the system to hold the excess of filth. Tumors that are open and run called ulcers are garbage cans that are so full they are running over.

CAUSE: Breaking the laws of health.

TREATMENT: Stop killing yourself. Cleanse the bowels with sea water, open up the kidneys with corn silk tea, take sweat baths to open up the skin. Get lots of fresh air. Get sun baths. Eat 2 meals a day, 8-9 a.m. and 3-4 p.m. of fruit at one meal and vegetables at the next. You will see these tumors go away.

HERBS: Corn silk tea. Blue vervain tea. Sea water treatment every morning.

TYPHOID FEVER—A Microbe

CAUSE: Spread in bowel movements, human manure from an infected person or a carrier. Water contaminated with human manure. Also from flies on food.

SYMPTOMS: Incubation 4-30 days. Diarrhea, sore belly, sound in ear, headache, languor, chills, nosebleed, temperature rise of 1 to 5 degrees. In 3 or 4 weeks perforation of intestines and death. Tongue gets small and belly large.

TREATMENT: Cleanse the bowels with 1/3 sea water and 2/3 hot water before breakfast. Put hot to the feet and cold to the abdomen. Give 1/2 lemon to 1 glass of water often. Give charcoal every hour and charcoal water to drink. Place a charcoal poultice over the abdomen.

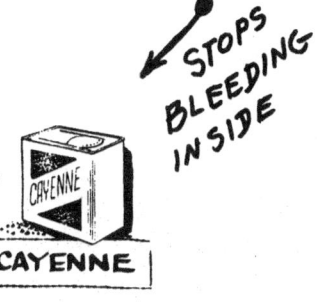

HERBS: Cayenne pepper, Golden sea, Root.

DIET: Rice water (natural unpolished), carrot juice, onion juice, vegetable juices of all kinds. Then fruit juices. Later use fruit and vegetable meals. Fruit at one meal and vegetables at the next.

TYPHUS FEVER—(tick fever in USA; SHIP FEVER, JAIL FEVER).

Usually transmitted from person to person by insect bites such as lice, ticks, fleas, wood ticks. Incubation period 4 to 14 days after bite.

SYMPTOMS: Sudden high fever. Weakness, chills. Bad headache, sometime convulsions. Red breaking out on skin in 4 or 5 days which go away in a few days. The spots of dark red are left on the skin, but not the face.

U

Blood may appear in the urine, bowel movements or even come up from the stomach. The disease reaches its peak at about two weeks. Here they die or slowly get well.

TREATMENT: Extremely cleanliness. Boil clothes and bed clothes. Delouse camp. Cleanse the bowels. Cleanse the skin. Low heat sweat baths. Give lots of charcoal water to drink hot or cold as may best suit the case.

Use cayenne pepper and golden seal root to stop bleeding and to heal. Take lots of sage tea bark and tops (old Indian remedy). Take charcoal every hour, mixed with olive oil and natural salt.

DIET: Rice water or barley water (natural), carrot juice, vegetable juices. Later on fruit.

U

ULCERS—DRUGS

"This is the effect of calomel.... It frequently manifests itself in tumors, ulcers, and cancers, years after it has been introduced into the system." HL 806.

"The disease, which the drug was given to cure may disappear, but only to reappear in a new form, such as skin diseases, ulcers, painful, diseased joints, and sometimes in a more dangerous and deadly form." HL 807.

ULCERS OF THE SKIN

A sore that will not heal and runs. Skin ulcers are an effort of nature to free the system from conditions that result from a violation of the laws of health. Ulcers may be found on most any part of the body, but very commonly on the feet and legs.

CAUSE: One of the worst cases was of a woman eating 9 meals a day, which included getting up at night several times to eat. The overload of food and that not the best, had clogged the system until these large running ulcers, which smelled very bad, were nature's only way to get rid of so much filth. Disobeying the 8 laws of health are the cause of ulcers.

TREATMENT: Stop killing yourself. Cleanse the bowels. Drink water. Sleep at night. Eat two meals a day 8-9 a.m. and 3-4 p.m. Eat fruit at one meal and vegetables at the next. Eat or drink nothing but water in between meals. Don't over-eat.

Don't try to heal up the ulcer. CLEAN UP THE FILTH IN THE BODY AND THE ULCER WILL HEAL UP ITSELF.

HERBS: Golden seal root powdered. Sorrel. Balsam or pine pitch.

UNDER WEIGHT—A SYMPTOM NOT A DISEASE.

But over-eating heads the list of thin people who overwise have not too much wrong with them. The body is overworked, disposing of more food than it can handle and so disposes of all of it. Eat 2 meals a day 8-9 a.m. and 3-4 p.m. Don't overeat, eat slowly and chew each mouthful 3 times as long as you do now. Eat fruit, grains, nuts, vegetables and sea weed. Eat fruit at one meal and vegetables at the next.

TREATMENT: Cleanse the bowels, take sweat baths, sun baths, fresh air, exercise, be happy.

HERBS: Golden seal. Cayenne pepper.

U

URINARY SYSTEM

"The bath is a soother of the nerves.... And acts beneficially on the kidneys and urinary organs." CH 104.

—DRINK LOTS OF WATER.

RETENTION OF URINE: Use corn silk tea. Princess pine. Juniper berries. Shave grass.
STONES: Smart weed tea. (Joint grass tea).
BLOODY: Cayenne pepper. Comfrey root tea, lemon water (no food) for 3-10 days.
DIFFICULT: Parsley tea. Princess Pine. Corn silk.
SCALDING: Corn silk tea. Shave grass. Slippery elm bark.

SITZ BATH

UTERUS
SEE: Women
HEMORRHAGE: Ice to the nipples. Cayenne taken in a little water.
ENLARGED: Unicorn root tea.
PROLAPSUS: Colombo (American) False unicorn root tea. White oak bark tea.
PAIN: Put on warm clothes on arms and legs. One of the greatest causes of female disease is unhealthful dress. "It is impossible for women to have, habitual, chilled limbs and cold feet, without some of the internal organs being congested. The many extra coverings over the chest and back and lower part of the body, induce the blood to these parts and the animal heat, thus retained, weakens and debilitates the delicate organs, and congestion and inflammation result." HL 551.

V

VARICOSE VEINS

RUB ON CASTOR OIL.

White oak bark tea. Rub on 3 times daily. Also drink some 3 times daily.

VINEGAR

"In my thirst they gave me vinegar to drink"—Ps. 69:20, 21. "But when He (Christ) had tasted it, He refused it." DA 746.

Vinegar stops healing. Even a few drops in the food. Use lemon juice and sea water instead. Vinegar is the lowest grade of alcohol. Don't use it.

VOMITING

BABIES: Sour—loosen clothes about belly. Stop over feeding. A 5 hour feeding schedule will often cure a lot of trouble. Give a little charcoal water, peppermint tea. Desert tea does wonders. Stop all food for a while. Cleanse the bowels.

PREGNANCY: Golden seal root tea. Peppermint tea. Desert tea. Marigold flowers tea. 1/2 tsp- every 2 hours. Red raspberry leaf tea.

VOMITING BLOOD: Give 1/2 tsp. cayenne pepper in a little cold water. Repeat if needed. See Ulcers.

GREEN BILE: Cleanse the bowels. Give a little cayenne pepper in water. Peppermint tea.

NEED TO VOMIT: (EMETIC) Drink a glass of lobelia seed tea. Salt water warm. Stick your finger down your throat. Follow with charcoal and water.

W

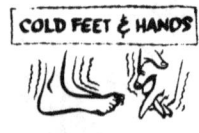

WAKEFULNESS

CAUSES: Nervous tension, worry, indecision, eating too late at night, head hot—feet cold.

TREATMENT: Take a cold enema, a cold sitz bath. Take a hot foot and leg bath. Relax your mind by trusting God. Pray. Read your Bible.

Babies that won't sleep: Take them outside and cool them off in the fresh air, then bring them in and warm them up. They will often go right off to sleep.

HERBS: Hop tea induces sleep. Catnip tea relaxes the nerves. Cayenne pepper equalizes the circulation.

WARTS

SYMPTOMS: A growth on the skin anywhere on the body, but usually on the hands or face. They come and go and no one seems to know why.

CAUSE: Unknown. Some think it may be caused by the mind.

TREATMENT: Bind on a poultice of garlic for a short time. Or apply milkweed juice. Sorrel poultice is very good in some cases.

WASP STINGS

SEE: Bee stings

W

WEAKNESS (EXCESSIVE AFTER SICKNESS)

Take a healthy egg beat it up in grape juice (unsweetened). This will give strength.

Oat tea. Bran water boiled 3/4 hour. Drink glassful twice a day.

WEAK PEOPLE

SYMPTOMS: No strength, pale face and ears. Walk very slowly often stooped forward. Dispirited, discouraged.

CAUSES: Lack of fresh air. Living indoors. No sunshine. Constipation. Lack of exercise. Masturbation. Self-abuse. Over sex indulgence. Tuberculosis. Anemia. Loss of blood. Eating a little food in between meals.

TREATMENT: Make a change in your living. Cleanse the bowels. Drink pure water. Breathe fresh air outside. Take a longer walk every day rain or shine. Take sweat baths. Eat some sea weed daily. Keep 6 hours in between meals.

WEIGHT—AVERAGE

Women, normal: 2 pounds per inch in height.

Men: About 2-1/2 pounds per inch in height.

Large or small bones make a difference.

WEIGHT LOSS

SEE: Tuberculosis, (T.B.), Cancer, Sex troubles. Find the cause. Which of the 8 laws of health need correction. Determine the cause.

W

WEIGHT OVER

SEE: Overweight

WHITES

SEE: Women

WHOOPING COUGH—CONTAGIOUS

SYMPTOMS: A childhood disease. Incubation about 8 or 9 days. Hard, deep coughing spells ending with a whopping sound. Onset something like a cold. Coughing so hard the face may get blue. Lasts for about 2 months.

TREATMENT: Cleanse the bowels. Take sweat baths. Eat only fruit, grains, nuts and vegetables, About 80% raw. Don't allow any eating in between meals. Nothing but water. Two meals a day best 8-9 a.m. and 3-4 p.m. Plenty of fresh air and sunshine.

HERBS: Red clover blossom tea. Raw potato juice with lemon juice.

WIDOW SPIDER BITE

SEE: Spider bite. Snake bite. "Snake bites and the sting of reptiles and poisonous insects could often be rendered harmless by the use of charcoal poultices." P of H 26.

WILL

"They should exercise the power of the will, rise above their aches and debility, and engage in useful employment, and forget that they have aching backs, sides, lungs and heads." HL 989.

W

"You have a determined will, which causes the mind to react upon the body, unbalancing the circulation, and producing congestion in certain organs, and you are sacrificing health to your feelings." HL 744.

"You are impressed that if you bathe, you will become chilly. The brain sends this intelligence to the nerves of the body, and the blood-vessels....Cannot perform their office and cause a reaction after the bath." HL 743.

WINE

"Never take tea, coffee, beer, wine, or any spirituous liquor. Water is the best liquid possible to cleanse the tissues." HL 673.

WOMEN

"Close confinement indoors makes women pale and feeble, and results in premature death." HL 256.

—INDOORS

"The tendency to feebleness and premature death decay in American women, is too evident to admit of a doubt and to no one thing is it so clearly traceable as to their habit of staying so closely in-doors. The aboriginal women of our country are as strong as the men." CT & BH 173.

W

—BRAINS

"A large class of women are content to hover over the stove, breathing impure air for 1/2 or 3/4 of the time, until the brain is heated and half benumbed. They should go out and exercise every day, even though some things indoors have to be neglected. They need the cool air to quiet distracted brains." HL 575.

"She should not call vitality unnecessarily to the surface to supply the want of sufficient clothing." 2T 382.

—CHILLED

"It is impossible for women to have, habitually, chilled limbs and cold feet, without some of the internal organs being congested." HL 551.

"There is but one woman in 1000 who clothes her limbs as she should. Women should clothe their limbs as thoroughly as do men." HL 548.

"More die as the result of following fashion than from all other causes." HL 275.

—DISEASES

"Half the diseases of women are caused by unhealthful dress." HL 544.

W

WOMB TIPPED

SYMPTOMS: Backache, constipation, menstrual pains, woman's being unable to become pregnant, or repeated abortions.

1. Use the knee chest exercise 2 or 3 times daily. Begin with 5 min. per day, increasing.
2. Follow the 8 laws of health.
3. Don't lift heavy things.
4. Take cold sitz baths between periods.

KNEE CHEST POSITION

—FALLING

1. White-oak bark douche.

Don't wear high heels.

WHITE OAK BARK

2. Douche of peach leaf, mullein, hops, tea works very well when all other remedies fail.
3. Keep arms and legs warm at all times.

KEEP ARMS AND LEGS WARM

4. Have at least 2 or 3 bowel movements daily.
5. Use the knee chest position 3 times daily.

—ULCERATION

1. Golden seal tea douche 2 or 3 times daily.
2. Oak bark tea douche twice daily
3. Keep arms and legs warm
4. Cleanse the bowels and be sure to have 2 or 3 bowel movements daily.

GOLDEN SEAL

WORK

"As a rule, the labor of the day should not be prolonged into the evening. Let parents devote the evenings to their families." CT & BH 65.

WORMS

Worms eat filth. Clean out the filth from the body and don't put in more filth and the worms leave because they have no food.

1. Drink nothing or eat nothing but pineapple juice for 4 days.
2. A diet of raw fruits, grains, nuts and vegetables and all the worms leave.
3. Hyssop—give 3 times daily before meals.
4. Male fern, powdered 4 oz. Mix with honey to form a paste. Give 1 or 2 tsp. at night. Laxative in morning of ocean water.

WORRY

Worry ends where faith in God begins. Faith in God ends where worry begins. Worry is a distrust of God. Worry is concentrating on the things you don't want. Worry is the inability to make a decision. Make a decision even if you are wrong. If you are wrong, change it. Think hard for 5 minutes and make a decision. "Labor is a source of happiness." PP 50.

WOUNDS—OLD

Wash with sage tea

WOUNDS—FRESH

Balsam pitch or pine pitch, best.

YELLOW SKIN

SEE: Jaundice

YELLOW FEVER

SYMPTOMS: Partial or general yellowness of the skin. Great tenderness or pain in the pit of the stomach. Bad cases, eyes intensely red. Pain in eye balls, back, and limbs. High fever, slow pulse.
CAUSE: Mosquito bites of Central and South America and other hot countries.
TREATMENT: Drink lots of water with charcoal. Cleanse the bowels, give sweat baths. Cold to the head and cold to the pit of the stomach. For vomiting drink warm water followed by ice water.
HERBS: Cayenne pepper in water often. Corn silk tea. Shave grass tea to open kidneys.

Z

ZOSTER
SEE: Shingles

We invite you to view the complete
selection of titles we publish at:

scan with your mobile
device to go directly
to our website

Please write or email us your praises, reactions, or
thoughts about this or any other book we publish at:

www.TEACHServices.com • (800) 367-1844

TEACH Services, Inc., titles may be purchased in bulk for
educational, business, fund-raising, or sales promotional use.
For information, please e-mail:

Finally if you are interested in seeing
your own book in print, please contact us at

We would be happy to review your manuscript for free.

www.ingramcontent.com/pod-product-compliance
Lightning Source LLC
Chambersburg PA
CBHW070919180426
43192CB00038B/1891